Strategies for
Differentiating
in the CONTENT
AREAS

**BEVERLY STRAYER
& TROY STRAYER**

█SCHOLASTIC

New York • Toronto • London • Auckland • Sydney
Mexico City • New Delhi • Hong Kong • Buenos Aires

Dedication

Critics and Critics row by row
Line the Plaza del Toro
But there is only one who knows
And that is he who fights the bull.

This poem was given to me by Dr. Eugene Segro two summers before his untimely death. Gene was instrumental in pushing me toward being a leader in our school district and being a driving force behind my use of differentiated instruction to better meet the needs of my students. This book is dedicated to his memory and the legacy he has left on everyone he had ever touched with his professionalism, his character, and his spirit.
Thank you, Gene. –T.S.

Acknowledgements

My first thank-you goes to my mother and co-author, who told me at a very early age I would be a teacher. It's funny how mothers know these things long before their children even have a clue. –T.S.

We'd like to thank our spouses, Lori and Lloyd, for standing by us and for their patience through the process of writing this book. Without their love and support this project would not have been possible.

We'd also like to thank our many colleagues who have tried and tested these strategies in their classrooms and who have provided us with invaluable feedback on their effectiveness and on areas of improvement. In particular, we'd like to thank Mr. Joel Hain, Mr. Jared Flay, Mr. Michael Dansberry, and Mrs. Deborah Kline for taking the initiative and risk to embrace these strategies in their classrooms. Also, we'd like to thank Mr. Craig Landis and Mr. James Bellenbaum for sharing their graphic organizers for this book.

Our thanks to our administrators Dr. Frank Herron, Mr. Kurt Fassnacht, and Mrs. Judy Eby for allowing us to experiment and for supporting us along the way.

Without our students there would be no book to write; we thank them for all that they have taught us over the years. They continue to shape us as people and as teachers.

Lastly, a huge thank you to our editor Sarah Longhi at Scholastic Teaching Resources for coming to our session at the National Middle School Conference in Philadelphia and for approaching us after the session about writing a book on differentiated instructional strategies. With her guidance and patience, we have felt at ease throughout the process and have had a wonderful learning experience. –B.S. & T.S.

Edited by Sarah Longhi

Cover design by Brian LaRossa
Interior design by Kelli Thompson
Illustrations for page 52 by Jason Robinson

ISBN-13 978-0-439-92920-2
ISBN-10 0-439-92920-2

1 2 3 4 5 6 7 8 9 10   31   15 14 13 12 11 10 09 08 07

Contents

The Strategies

Introduction

How fantastic! You have decided to differentiate instruction in your middle school classroom. This guide will be invaluable as you begin or continue your journey of differentiation. The flexible strategies contained in this book are easy to create, easy to use, and will meet the many, varied needs of your middle school students.

In 1995, we began our differentiation journey after hearing a presentation by Carol Ann Tomlinson of the University of Virginia. Tomlinson inspired us to begin to differentiate our instruction to better reach all of our students. As we struggled through that first year, we found that many of the strategies we tried were labor intensive, and this struggle pushed us to search for equally effective strategies that required a manageable preparation time. Over the last eleven years, we have identified and adapted truly "low-prep" strategies that engage middle schoolers in learning and get a stamp of approval from our colleagues, who find them user-friendly and effective. Our top eight strategies are the subject of this book.

What Exactly Is Differentiation?

When we attempt to differentiate instruction in our classrooms, we begin with the basics: *content, process,* and *product.* Content refers to what students should know, understand, and be able to do, and is informed by our state and national standards and the curriculum adopted by our local school boards. Process is the "how" of differentiation, including the strategies, activities, and procedures that help students make sense of and take ownership of their learning. The product is the end result of the learning process; it shows how students have demonstrated and extended what they've learned.

While keeping in mind the content we want to teach, as well as options for teaching that content and for having students show what they've learned, we need to take into account the way our students will impact the decisions we'll make. Their readiness, interests, and learning profiles also affect how we differentiate our teaching.

By *readiness* we mean the background information, skills, and abilities a child brings to the learning. Identifying your students' readiness levels enables you to design appropriate lessons and activities that are challenging and relevant to all learners in your classroom. For example, following a pre-assessment quiz on body systems in an eighth-grade health class, you observe that five students demonstrated mastery of the content while fifteen students did not answer any questions correctly. You would need to account for the different levels of readiness in the classroom by differentiating the content you present: five students will certainly benefit from reading more in-depth material than the prepared unit provides. You might also consider other process and product options to push these learners forward, such as using enriching anchor activities (Chapter 1) or having them produce a more extensive research presentation than a standard one-page summary presentation at the end of the unit.

When we tap into the *interests* of our students—another key to differentiating instruction—we build bridges between their personal lives and our specific content areas, providing a source of intrinsic motivation. Learning takes place because the students want to—not because they have to. For example, in a seventh-grade technology education unit on manufacturing and production, you decide to change the standard assignment: having students design and market to a general audience a product you've chosen. This time you allow students to design a product that they've chosen and market it to their peers. Students get excited and feel empowered to learn because they can choose their own products based on their interest in the topic. You might also give some students more structured steps in a checklist format, to ensure that they can manage their own learning process better.

The final aspect to consider when differentiating—the student's *learning profile*—includes the student's

- preferred learning style(s) (visual, auditory, tactile, or kinesthetic);
- areas of strength in the multiple intelligences framework (visual-spatial, logical-mathematical, verbal-linguistic, intrapersonal, interpersonal, musical-rhythmic, bodily-kinesthetic, or naturalistic);
- grouping preferences (individual, small group, or large group); and
- environmental preferences (size of work space, amount of sensory stimulation, and so on).

Elements of Differentiation

Instruction

CONTENT
What students should know, understand, and be able to do

PROCESS
How students make sense of or take ownership of their learning

PRODUCT
The work students create to demonstrate and extend their learning

Student Needs

READINESS
Schema, skills, and abilities students bring to their learning

INTERESTS
Topics, ideas, trends, and issues that most appeal to students

LEARNING PROFILE
The unique way each student learns

You may differentiate your instruction based on any one of these factors or any combination of factors (Tomlinson, 1999). Understanding how our students learn best is fundamental to their success in our content-area classes. For example, in a lesson on fighting styles in the French and Indian War, you decide to use a kinesthetic model for a group of sports-oriented students to contrast the fighting style of the English with that of the Native Americans. You divide your class in half, show them how each side would "fire" paper balls, representing bullets or weapons, and lay down basic ground rules for safety during the enactment. The class then role-plays a battle scene with the first group "fighting" in the traditional European style and the second group "fighting" guerrilla style. They soon notice that the English side takes the biggest hit; they have experienced how the two styles heavily influenced the early stages of the war in a way they won't forget. By incorporating these types of activities, we are activating multiple learning styles and intelligences in one lesson and addressing many students' needs in one learning episode.

Using This Book

This book is designed to accomplish the following goals:

- Identify and describe differentiated instructional strategies that have proven to be successful in a middle school setting. You'll find ideas and tips for adapting them to different content areas.
- Provide examples of student work to demonstrate how a strategy looks in action. Please use these examples to think through the ways your students might approach the assignment and to troubleshoot any problems they may encounter. You may also want to present these samples as models that students may refer to before they tackle the assignment.
- Provide activities that are respectful (appropriate to students' readiness) and meaningful (address students' interests and learning profiles) so that all your learners can experience success in the classroom.

The chart on pages 7 and 8 describes the strategies that are introduced in this book and shows how they can be used to meet your goals and address students' needs.

Differentiated Strategy	Instructional Focus	Student Needs Addressed	Strategy Description
Anchoring Student Learning	Content	Readiness Interest Learning Styles	This strategy helps you answer the question "What do I do now?" from students who have a firm grasp of the topic and have completed an assignment ahead of their peers. Anchor activities provide productive, relevant tasks for these students.
Note-Taking	Content Process	Interest Learning Styles	This set of strategies helps you teach note-taking in disguise. You'll find four engaging formats for presenting information to demonstrate content mastery.
Using Graphic Organizers	Content Process Product	Readiness Interest Learning Styles	Tired of using Venn diagrams? These graphic organizers offer students new ways to represent their learning visually and can be tiered for different skill levels.
Cubing	Product	Readiness Interest Learning Styles	Cubing assignments develop students' conceptual under-standing of a given topic and challenge them to process information at higher levels. Draw on Bloom's Taxonomy or Gardner's Multiple Intelligence framework to offer students six ways to examine a topic.
R.A.F.T.-ing	Product	Interest	Whenever students look at a topic from a new perspective, they activate new pathways to understanding the material—and they learn it better. R.A.F.T.-ing presents students with an opportunity not only to choose their product, but also to present a topic from a unique perspective. It's a great way for you to check that students really comprehend key concepts and information about the topic you're teaching.

Differentiated Strategy	Instructional Focus	Student Needs Addressed	Strategy Description
Working With Choice Boards	Product	Readiness Interest Learning Styles	Students who choose their learning activities are motivated to perform at higher levels. Choice Boards provide options for completing in-class assignments or culminating unit assessments. They are easy to create and can be simple to assess.
Terminology Tactics	Content Process	Interest Learning Styles	Vocabulary study does not have to be boring and routine. These three strategies enhance students' ability to understand and retain terminology they must learn in order to meet the content area standards.
Providing Closure	Process	Readiness Learning Styles	Since Madeline Hunter's research on effective teaching in 1979, teachers have included closure as part of the daily lesson plan. We describe eight ways to help students show what they've learned at the end of your daily lessons.

There is no limit to what you can do with these strategies. To ensure your success, we've added the following support in each chapter: examples of how the strategy was used in our classrooms, a step-by-step procedure, companion reproducibles and templates, ideas for applying the strategy across content areas, and student work samples. Most strategies also include a ready-to-use rubric for assessment.

Whether you have little or no training in differentiated instruction or have been implementing it for years, you can turn to any strategy in this book to enhance your instruction and scaffold learning for all students in your classroom. It is our hope that using these strategies helps you along your differentiation journey toward success and growth for your students and for you.

CHAPTER 1

Anchoring Student Learning

CONTENT OBJECTIVE:

Students practice, review, or extend what they know about a specific topic.

DIFFERENTIATION APPROACH:

Vary the products students choose by tapping into readiness, interest, or learning style.

In a truly differentiated classroom, students progress at different rates through the content and materials you offer. To anchor students' learning about the current unit or topic, you can provide additional learning activities for students who finish the class assignment early. The goal is to enhance and solidify their understanding by engaging them further with the content. Anchoring is also a helpful differentiation management strategy: as students who need more time are working on required assignments and projects, others, who are finished, may choose an anchor activity. There is no need for anyone to ask you, "What should I do now?" because in a differentiated classroom, anchor activities are always available for those who are finished early. Having students immersed in valuable activities, rather than busywork, also frees you up to work with small groups of students or individuals.

"You are never finished learning" is the mantra of a differentiated classroom. Anchor activities must be self-paced, meaningful, content-driven tasks that students can complete independently during a unit, week, grading period, or longer period of time. These activities provide meaningful tasks that remediate, offer practice, or extend students' learning.

Whether they are tiered to meet the needs of different readiness levels or designed to appeal to multiple intelligences, anchor activities may be used as formative assessment during a unit of study or as a summative assessment with students of higher ability who are able to complete extended tasks independently. Assessment tools, including a student checklist and a scoring rubric, are included in this chapter.

Materials

- Anchor Activity Ideas (page 12)
- Anchor Activities template (page 13)
- Anchor Activity Checklist (page 17) (optional)
- Anchor Activity Rubric (page 18) (optional)

Procedure

1. Guided by the objective you want your students to learn, use the activity template to write at least three anchor activities that can be completed during the two or three weeks of a unit of study. You may want to review the examples of anchor assignments in science, math, social studies, and reading on pages 14 and 15. For example, as you complete a unit on light and sound, one of your anchor activities might be to create a demonstration of refraction to share with the class. During a unit on the Revolutionary War, one of your anchor activities might be to make a time-line of major battles of the war. In math, an ongoing anchor activity might involve writing word problems for classmates to solve. (See the example on page 16.)

2. Introduce and explain to the class the anchor activities you've developed and model how to complete each one. Be clear about your expectations, establishing a policy for student accountability and assessment. Make sure you also set clear ground rules and procedures for this independent work. For example, you may have a rule that students must check with you before beginning anchor activities. This helps you monitor the work of students who may hurry through required work to get to a favorite anchor activity.

3. Set the anchor activities with all the necessary materials in a place in the room that is readily accessible to students.

4. Have specific times or stopping points at which students should check in with you during the course of the activity. This will help you gauge whether students are using their time wisely. We recommend a weekly check-in with students.

In our classroom, we are never *finished* learning. Learning is a process that continues your entire life . . . Try an **anchor activity!**

A sign that encourages students to stay engaged with their learning also serves as a visual reminder of what to do next and where to go for the assignment. We hang this sign by the anchor assignment sheets.

5. Before students turn in any anchor activity, have them use criteria to evaluate whether the assignment meets expectations. You might want to use the Anchor Activities Checklist (or a checklist you've created), to help students target areas to improve and revise before they hand in the assignment. If you choose not to use the checklist, give students the Anchor Activity Rubric (or a rubric you've developed) before they begin the activity. Students can use the rubric to plan for and later refine and improve their activity. Both you and your students can score the activities with the rubric.

Anchor Activity Ideas

Teacher-Created Anchors

The anchors you create may include activity formats that you already assign regularly, such as crossword puzzles that you generate on the computer. These often have a self-checking component and require less explanation and guidance.

Vocabulary concentration

Geoboard challenges

Content crossword puzzles

WebQuests

Map activities

Jeopardy

Magazine articles

Word finds

Tangram puzzles

Logic puzzles

Listening-center activities

Newspaper searches

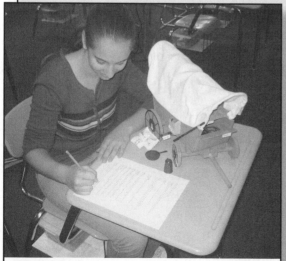

Wrapping up an anchor activity on Conestoga Wagons

Student-Created Anchors

These prompts for student-generated activities are more open-ended and will require some modeling. However, once students are familiar with it, you can recycle the format in a new unit with ease.

Conduct research on the topic.

Write a review of a magazine article.

Create a bulletin board.

Write a one-act play.

Write a commercial.

Write a journal entry from a specific figure or point of view.

Have a book talk with a partner.

Create a crossword puzzle with key vocabulary.

Develop a Jeopardy-style game.

Develop interview questions.

Create a PowerPoint™ presentation.

Create a board game.

Make a timeline.

Illustrate a picture or draw a diagram.

Make a story map.

Write a letter to a character or historical figure.

Make word stars.

Write a poem or rap.

Create math word problems.

Write in your writer's notebook.

Create a cartoon strip.

Design a diorama.

Make a video.

Anchor Activities

for _____

Choose an anchor activity from the list below that will help you show what you know about _____. Keep in mind that you will need several class periods to complete the activity. Take your time and do your best.

⚓ _____

_____

_____

MATERIALS:

⚓ _____

_____

_____

MATERIALS:

⚓ _____

_____

_____

MATERIALS:

Anchor Activities

Science: Physics of Light and Sound

Students who finish class work early may choose an anchor activity from the list below to extend their learning about light and sound. They may take independent work time over the course of several class periods to complete the activity. (Materials other than paper and pencil are listed.)

- Draw a picture to show how we see colors.

- Create a cartoon that defines light and/or sound through the dialogue of the characters.

- Use a slinky to show how sound waves travel and draw a diagram using the slinky as your model. Include labels and brief explanations to make the diagram clear.
  Materials: slinky

- Create a ten-note song using four glasses of water and a spoon as your instrument. Draw the glasses, showing the water level in each and explain how you used them to create a song.
  Materials: set of glasses, metal spoon, water

Math: Fractions and Percents

These anchor activities help students extend their learning about fractions and percents. (Materials other than paper and pencil are listed.)

- Create and solve three multistep word problems dealing with percentages and fractions. Record your solutions and answers on the back of the page.

- Using the grocery advertisement provided, create a shopping list of at least ten items. At the bottom of the list, total your item cost and then compute the cost with a 30 percent discount off all items at that store.
  Materials: grocery advertisement

- Take one of the recipes for cookies provided and double it so that you can make cookies for more people (list the new unit measure for each ingredient). After completing this task, cut the original recipe in half (again, list the new unit measure for each ingredient).
  Materials: copies of cookie recipes

Anchor Activities

Social Studies: Westward Expansion

These anchor activities help students extend their learning about westward expansion. (Each activity requires paper and pencil.)

- Write a chant to explain westward expansion. Be sure to mention several causes and their effects.

- Using a Venn diagram, compare and contrast the Mexican War and our current war in Iraq.

- Research the Donner Party experience. Write a different ending to this tragic event, showing how the party might have encountered different challenges or made different decisions.

- Research five ghost towns of the West. What happened to those towns to cause them to "disappear"? List as many causes as you can find for each.

Reading: Plot Development

These anchor activities help students extend their learning about how a plot unfolds. (Materials other than paper and pencil are listed.)

- For each plot point in the story you're reading, pick a noun that represents something, someone, or an idea that's important to the action. On a paper folded into six sections illustrate each noun in order of the plot points (one illustration per section).
  Materials: sheet of construction paper

- Complete a story map of your current independent reading book.
  Materials: Story Map template

- Write a short letter to a character from your current book warning him or her about key upcoming events he or she may have to face. Include your advice on how to manage the situation.

- If your book does not have chapter titles, write them to reflect key parts of the plot. If it has chapter titles, write new ones, closely focused on the action.

Anchor Activity: Math

(Fractions and Percents assignment, page 14)

ASSIGNMENT NOTES:

These problems come from Jessica, an advanced math student who has a solid understanding of the relationship between percentages and fractions. She opted for this anchor assignment when she'd finished her required work and checked in with me. After Jessica turned in the word problems, I typed them up and used them as an anchor activity for other students to solve (see answer page by Brady below). Jessica was responsible for checking their solutions. This process encouraged others to complete the same anchor activity with little or no additional work on my part—they knew they'd have a chance to do the questioning and the checking.

Anchor Word Problems

Problem 1: Jessica wants to buy a jacket that is on sale at 25% off. The original price was $41.50. She has $33.00 with her. Does she have enough money for the jacket? If she does and she buys the jacket, how much money will she have left?

Problem 2: John wants to buy a pair of sneakers that are on sale for 20% off and a new pair of jeans at 25% off. The original prices are $69.99 for the sneakers and $26.88 for the jeans. What would John's total bill be if he bought both on sale? If John had $100.00, would he have enough money to buy two pair of jeans?

Problem 3: Sue got 27 out of 30 questions right on her first math test, 34 out of 40 right on her second math test, and 23 out of 25 right on her last test. What is her current math average in percentage? What percentage would she have to have on her next test to get an A?

Answer to Problem 1

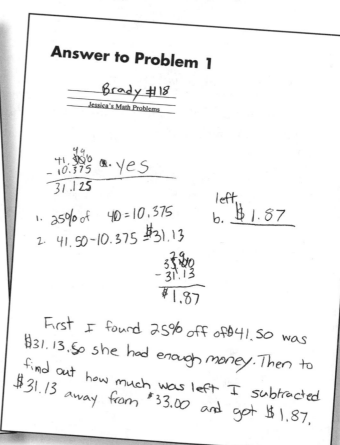

Brady #18

Jessica's Math Problems

a. yes

b. $1.87 left

1. 25% of 40 = 10.375
2. 41.50 − 10.375 = 31.13

$1.87

First I found 25% off of $41.50 was $31.13. So she had enough money. Then to find out how much was left I subtracted $31.13 away from $33.00 and got $1.87.

⚓ ANCHOR ACTIVITY CHECKLIST

Name _____ Date _____

⚓ Anchor activity _____

Accuracy
❏ I've checked the information presented in my activity carefully. It is correct.

❏ I need to check the following parts: _____

_____

Completion
❏ I completed the entire activity.

❏ These are steps I still need to complete: _____

_____

Focus
❏ I stuck to the activity described in the directions. _____

_____

❏ I did some parts differently. (Explain.) _____

_____

Mechanics
❏ For any written parts of the activity, I checked punctuation, spelling, and grammar.

❏ For any mathematical parts of the activity, I've double checked my calculations and shown my work.

❏ I still need to check the following mechanics: _____

_____

Neatness
❏ The overall quality of this anchor activity is the best work I can do.

❏ I could still improve the following: _____

_____

Changes made:
❏

❏

❏

❏   Date turned in: _____

Anchor Activity Rubric

Assignment Traits	←				
Accuracy Is the information presented in the activity correct? Are there gaps in the information?	5	4	3	2	1
	Comments:				
Completion Is the activity complete? Were there steps that proved challenging?	5	4	3	2	1
	Comments:				
Focus Did the student stick to the activity described in the directions? Did he or she fully develop the chosen activity in a detailed or creative way?	5	4	3	2	1
	Comments:				
Mechanics Did the writing and/or computation contain few errors? Did the student check punctuation, spelling, and grammar?	5	4	3	2	1
	Comments:				
Neatness Is the overall quality of this anchor activity the student's best work?	5	4	3	2	1
	Comments:				

Grade (based on levels attained for each criterion)

Scoring key

25–24 = A+	19 = B+	14 = C+	10 = D
23–21 = A	18–16 = B	13–12 = C	9 = D–
20 = A–	15 = B–	11 = C–	

Assessment guide

5 = Advanced
4 = Proficient
3 = Basic
2 = Below Basic
1 = Novice

Date

Name

CHAPTER 2

Using Graphic Organizers

CONTENT OBJECTIVE:

Students organize the information they have learned in a graphic format.

DIFFERENTIATION APPROACH:

Vary the process students use to demonstrate knowledge based on readiness and/or learning style.

Middle school students often need help to process and prioritize the detailed information we present in content areas; it is our task to provide a way to make the content manageable, organized, and easy to understand. We can use graphic organizers—visual representations of content, concepts, or information—to show students how we organize information and think in our disciplines. For instance, rather than limit students' understanding of the military impact of the Civil War with tasks that primarily involve memorization and basic recall of names, battle dates, and statistics, we can assign students a concept map that helps them learn about two or three key battles that affected the outcome of the war. This type of work ensures that students are processing information, making sense of it, discriminating essential from nonessential details, and effectively communicating that information to others in a structured way.

There are important reasons for using graphic organizers to differentiate your instruction. First, in a visually accessible format information becomes less cluttered and easier to work with. This format appeals to students with strong visual-spatial and logical-mathematical intelligences. Students with learning difficulties or reading problems also may handle information better when it is graphically organized; they can demonstrate their learning without being hindered by complex writing or reading tasks.

Second, reading, writing, and communication skills improve when students think critically and analytically. The process of putting information into a graphic organizer is quite different from writing essays or answering multiple-choice questions. Organizers help students think strategically and communicate that thinking in writing. Using a variety of organizers in your teaching—hierarchical, conceptual, sequential, and cyclical—allows you to differentiate based on process.

Any graphic organizer may be assessed for a grade using the rubric provided in this chapter. Instead of giving a unit test of essay questions that demand a lot of composition time, for example, you may want to try an organizer that targets the same material instead. If students can successfully complete the organizer, you will know that they have not only learned the information but have also internalized and organized it into meaningful chunks.

Materials

- Copies of the graphic organizer of your choice (or an overhead transparency from which students may copy the format). We include several in this chapter: Concept Map (page 22), Reading Road Map (pages 23–24), and Essay Organizer (page 25)
- Graphic Organizer Checklist (page 31)
- Graphic Organizer Rubric (page 32)

Procedure

1. Keeping in mind the objective or standard you want your students to demonstrate, choose the graphic organizer that will best help them organize the information or ideas. For example, a Concept Map will help students summarize and organize information they have learned from lectures, discussions, and research (see the leveled variations on page 26). The Essay Organizer serves as a prewriting map of ideas for an informational essay on any topic (see examples on page 27). As you begin a unit of study, you may choose to provide a Reading Road Map for students to complete as they read and process a required textbook passage (see the example on page 29).

2. To tier or level the organizers for different readiness needs in your class, consider what response or information would satisfy grade-level expectations. Make sure that the on-level organizer you shape asks this appropriately. Provide students who need more support with a scaffolded version of the on-level organizer. For example, you might fill in some sections or reduce the amount of information that's required. You might also design a more advanced organizer for students who need a more challenging task. (Consider tasks that require more analysis, evaluation, and synthesis, that involve more steps, or that deal with more-complex information.) To see how you might make simple adjustments to level the organizers in this chapter, see the tiered examples of the Concept Map (page 28) and Essay Organizer (page 30).

3. Using an example on the overhead projector, model how to use the graphic organizer with the class. Be clear about your expectations for the assignment: you want students' best work. To make sure students are comfortable with one organizer before introducing another, do not introduce more than one organizer at a time.

4. To scaffold instruction, have students work in small groups or partnerships to complete an example of the organizer you have just modeled. Circulate and assist groups as needed.

5. Assign students to complete an organizer for independent work when you are certain that they understand the task. This is the time to work with small groups to introduce a leveled organizer that challenges them appropriately.

6. Before students turn in a graphic organizer, have them evaluate the assignment. You may want to provide them with the Graphic Organizer Checklist (or a checklist you've created) to target areas to improve and revise. Or you may give students the Graphic Organizer Rubric (or a rubric you've developed) before they begin the activity. Students can use the rubric to plan for and later refine and improve their activity.

7. Score the completed organizers with the rubric.

Concept Map

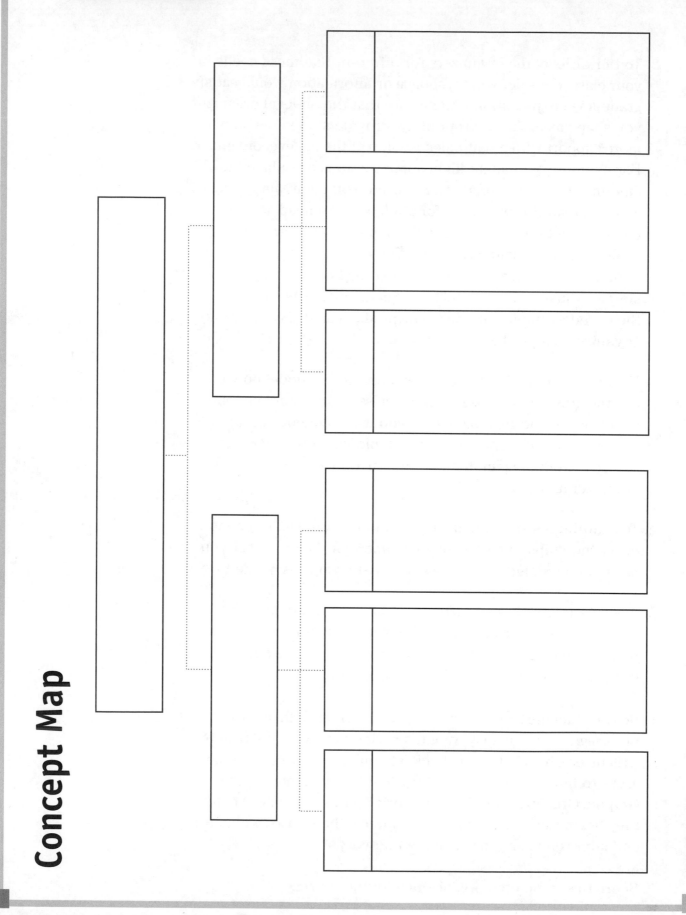

Reading Road Map

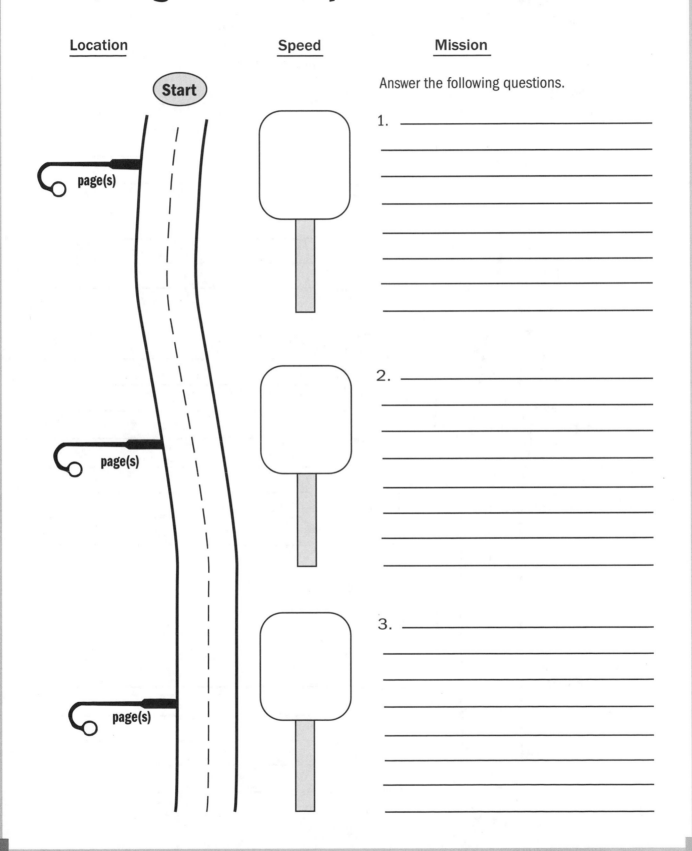

Location

Start

page(s)

page(s)

page(s)

Speed

Mission

Answer the following questions.

1. _____

_____

_____

_____

_____

_____

2. _____

_____

_____

_____

_____

_____

_____

3. _____

_____

_____

_____

_____

_____

_____

Reading Road Map

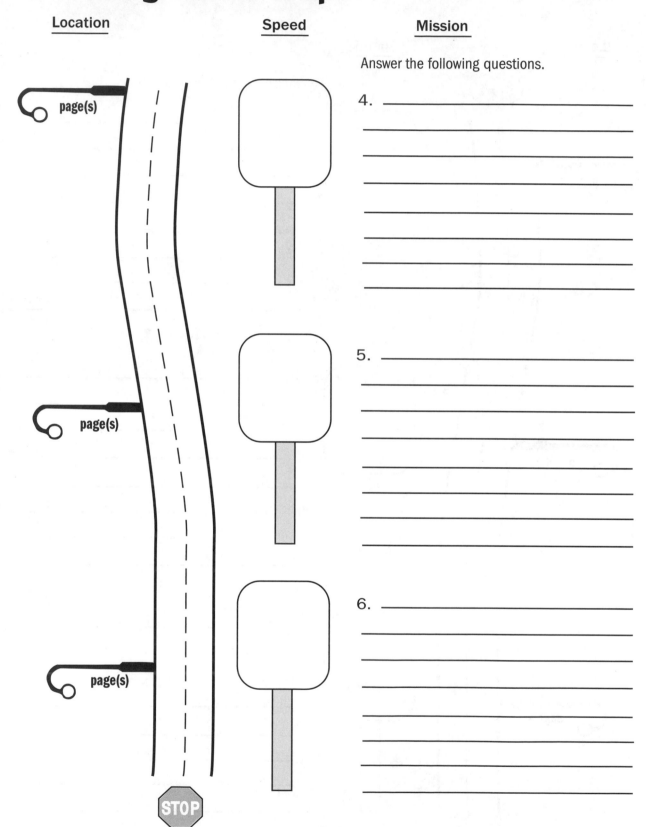

Location

Speed

Mission

Answer the following questions.

page(s)

4. _____

_____

_____

_____

_____

_____

_____

page(s)

5. _____

_____

_____

_____

_____

_____

_____

page(s)

6. _____

_____

_____

_____

_____

_____

STOP

Essay Organizer

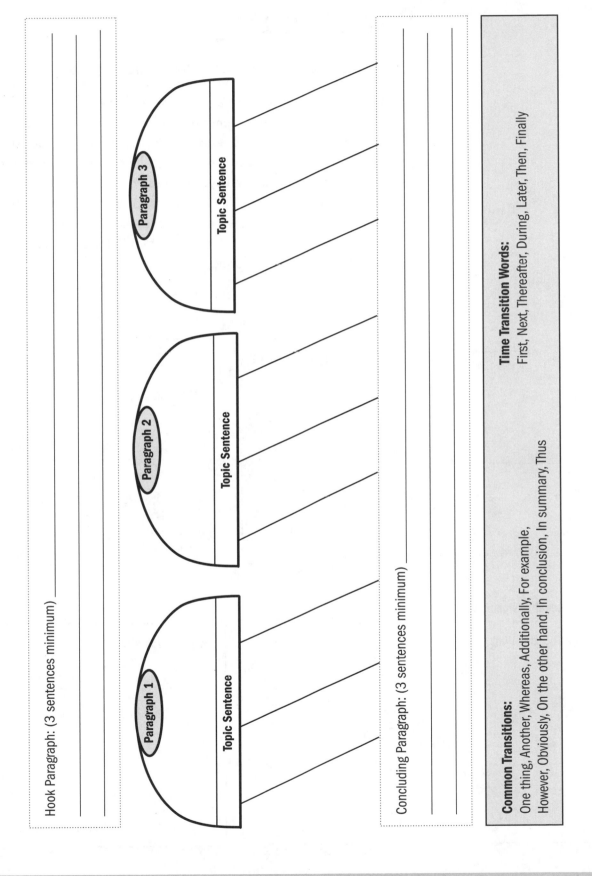

Hook Paragraph: (3 sentences minimum)

Paragraph 1

Topic Sentence

Paragraph 2

Topic Sentence

Paragraph 3

Topic Sentence

Concluding Paragraph: (3 sentences minimum)

Time Transition Words:
First, Next, Thereafter, During, Later, Then, Finally

Common Transitions:
One thing, Another, Whereas, Additionally, For example, However, Obviously, On the other hand, In conclusion, In summary, Thus

Concept Map

Social Studies: The American Revolution (tiered)

Working on a Concept Map organizer that is appropriately leveled allows each student to demonstrate his or her understanding of a big concept in the same reading assignment. During our study of the Revolutionary War, I wanted my fifth graders to be aware of the differences between the Loyalists and Patriots: why they chose the side they did, what their beliefs were, and some famous people on each side. I used only two detail boxes for students needing the most support and added an additional subtopic for students who were able to grasp more information.

On-Level Assignment

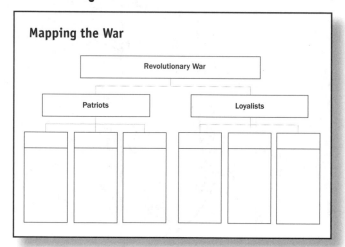

Below-Level Assignment

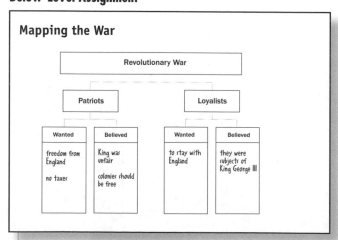

Above-Level Assignment

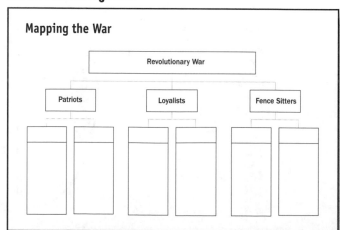

Essay Organizer

Science: Informational Essay

Across the board, middle schoolers' writing tends to lack organization. Before students complete any content-area writing, we have them use an organizer to help them process and structure the information. These tiered essay organizers allow science students at different readiness levels to gather information and organize their research notes to write an essay, in this case on fungi. As the difficulty of the organizers increases, the advanced students are asked to use more sophisticated transitions and supply additional information. At the same time, students aren't concerned about having different assignments than their peers because all the organizers are structured in the same way.

On-Level Assignment

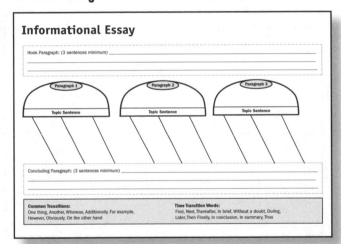

Below-Level Assignment

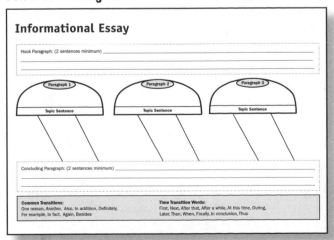

Above-Level Assignment

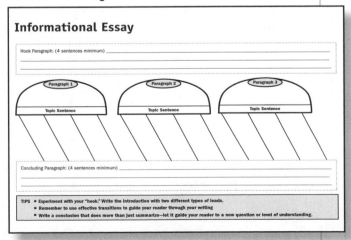

Concept Map: Social Studies

(American History, American Revolution assignment, page 26)

ASSIGNMENT NOTES:

Our objective was to understand the beliefs and backgrounds of key groups in the Revolutionary War. For students working below level and on level, it was enough to know at least two main differences between the groups. For the advanced students, it was important that they also knew of the "fence-sitters" and the impact they had on the Revolution. Even in the below-level assignment shown here, students were guided to find two key characteristics about each group.

On-Level Assignment

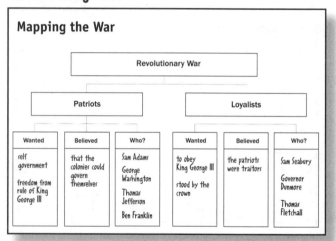

Below-Level Assignment

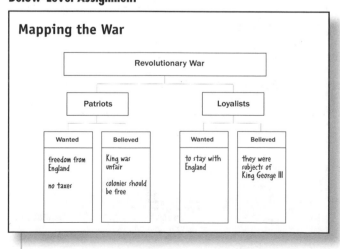

Above-Level Assignment

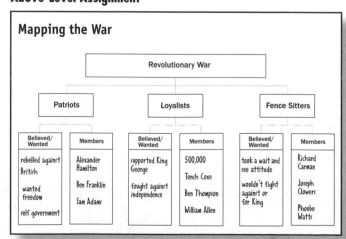

Reading Road Map: Science

(Earth Sciences, Oceans)

ASSIGNMENT NOTES:

This Reading Road Map organizer was designed for use in an inclusion class. It helps students who need support to locate important information while reading assigned content-area material. This particular organizer helped students navigate "Oceans," a selection from a seventh-grade science textbook, which was challenging for many of our students. It highlights the main points and prompts them to fill in key ideas as they read. To prepare this organizer, we completed the Location, Speed, and Mission columns based on the main ideas of the reading, and structured the space appropriately to guide the type and length of response students gave.

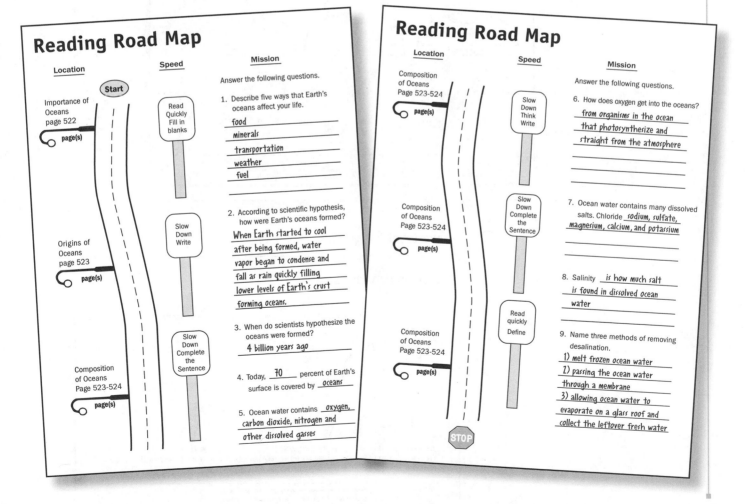

Essay Organizer: Science

(Life Sciences, Fungi)

ASSIGNMENT NOTES:

These organizers were designed for a diverse group of students who were preparing to write informative essays on fungi. In the example on the top, a student needing extra support filled in the organizer during small-group work with teacher guidance. Meanwhile, other students were able to work independently or in pairs with their research notes to complete the above-level organizer. Both met prewriting goals.

Below-Level Assignment

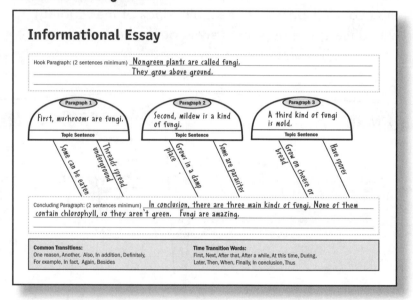

Informational Essay

Hook Paragraph: (2 sentences minimum) _Nongreen plants are called fungi. They grow above ground._

Paragraph 1
First, mushrooms are fungi.
Topic Sentence
Some can be eaten
Threads spread underground

Paragraph 2
Second, mildew is a kind of fungi.
Topic Sentence
Grows in a damp place
Some are parasites

Paragraph 3
A third kind of fungi is mold.
Topic Sentence
Grow on cheese or bread
Have spores

Concluding Paragraph: (2 sentences minimum) _In conclusion, there are three main kinds of fungi. None of them contain chlorophyll, so they aren't green. Fungi are amazing._

Common Transitions:
One reason, Another, Also, In addition, Definitely, For example, In fact, Again, Besides

Time Transition Words:
First, Next, After that, After a while, At this time, During, Later, Then, When, Finally, In conclusion, Thus

Above-Level Assignment

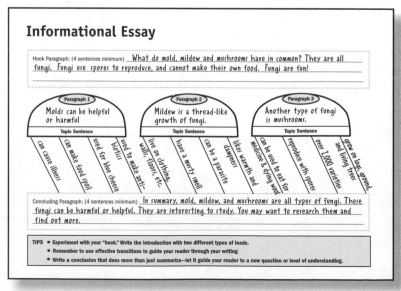

Informational Essay

Hook Paragraph: (4 sentences minimum) _What do mold, mildew and mushrooms have in common? They are all fungi. Fungi use spores to reproduce, and cannot make their own food. Fungi are fun!_

Paragraph 1
Molds can be helpful or harmful
Topic Sentence
can cause illness
can make food spoil
used for blue cheese
used to make anti-biotics

Paragraph 2
Mildew is a thread-like growth of fungi.
Topic Sentence
live on clothing, walls, floors, etc.
have a musty smell
can be a parasite
likes warmth and dampness

Paragraph 3
Another type of fungi is mushrooms.
Topic Sentence
can be used to eat for medicine & dying wool
reproduce with spores
over 1,000 varieties
grow on logs, ground, and living trees

Concluding Paragraph: (4 sentences minimum) _In summary, mold, mildew, and mushrooms are all types of fungi. These fungi can be harmful or helpful. They are interesting to study. You may want to research them and find out more._

TIPS • Experiment with your "hook." Write the introduction with two different types of leads.
• Remember to use effective transitions to guide your reader through your writing.
• Write a conclusion that does more than just summarize—let it guide your reader to a new question or level of understanding.

GRAPHIC ORGANIZER CHECKLIST

Name _____ Date _____

Graphic organizer title _____

Content
❏ I've included the most important information about my topic/subject.

❏ There's something else I could add: _____

_____

_____

Accuracy
❏ I've checked the information presented in the organizer. It is correct.

❏ I still need to check some facts. I'm going to check the following: _____

_____

Completion
❏ I filled in the entire organizer.

❏ There are still unfinished parts. I need help with: _____

_____

_____

Focus
❏ I stuck to the activity described in the directions.

❏ I did it differently. (Explain.) _____

_____

_____

Neatness
❏ The organizer is neat enough to read.

❏ I need to recopy it so it's legible.

Changes made:
❏

❏

❏

❏   Date turned in: _____

Graphic Organizer Rubric

Date _____

Name _____

Assignment Traits	←				
Content Does the organizer include the most important information about the topic/subject? Were there noticeable gaps in the information?	5	4	3	2	1
	Comments:				
Accuracy Is the information in the organizer accurate?	5	4	3	2	1
	Comments:				
Completion Is the organizer filled in completely/adequately?	5	4	3	2	1
	Comments:				
Focus The student stuck to the assigned activity.	5	4	3	2	1
	Comments:				
Neatness The organizer is neat enough to read and represents the student's best work.	5	4	3	2	1
	Comments:				

Grade (based on levels attained for each criterion)

Scoring key				Assessment guide
25–24 = A+	19 = B+	14 = C+	10 = D	5 = Advanced
23–21 = A	18–16 = B	13–12 = C	9 = D–	4 = Proficient
20 = A–	15 = B–	11 = C–		3 = Basic
				2 = Below Basic
				1 = Novice

CHAPTER 3

Cubing

CONTENT OBJECTIVE:
Students demonstrate in detail what they have learned during a unit of study.

DIFFERENTIATION APPROACH:
Vary the content students learn and/or the products they produce by tuning in to their readiness to learn, interests, and learning preferences.

With cubing assignments, rolling a large paper die turns up a question or a learning task, and students eagerly watch to find out what their assignment is. A motivational alternative to the traditional test or worksheet, cubing is structured to give students the opportunity to analyze a topic from six different perspectives and show what they've learned about the topic in a creative way. Cubes are versatile: You have the option of differentiating tasks according to students' readiness, interests, or learning styles. For example, cubes that are leveled based on Bloom's Taxonomy can help students work with information at the right skill level, and cubes that offer activities designed to tap specific intelligences can motivate students to be invested in learning about the target topic.

Student's work from cubing activities may be used for a formative or summative assessment of a unit study. Using cubing as a formative assessment tool can help you determine areas in which students need more instruction and to determine who is ready to move on to an enrichment activity or anchor activity (see Chapter 1).

e learned about cubing at a staff development workshop years ago, and since then we've used it in almost all of our units of study—from fractions to westward expansion. Students enjoy the process of rolling the cube to see how they will demonstrate their knowledge of a lesson or unit. We also find that cubing increases their sense of ownership of the content by providing some options about the product they'll create and the process they'll follow, while also promoting higher-level thinking skills based on Bloom's Taxonomy.

Materials

- Bloom's Taxonomy List of Activity Options (page 36–37)
- Multiple Intelligences Menu of Activity Ideas (page 38)
- Cube template (page 39)
- Think Dots template (page 40)
- Cubing Checklist (page 44)
- Cubing Rubric (page 45)

Procedure

1. Choose an objective or set of objectives from your current unit for which you want students to demonstrate mastery.

2. If you are differentiating the assignment by readiness, determine the appropriate grouping for your students based on their skill level (making groups at two or three levels is most manageable). For each readiness group, create a set of six questions or tasks that will help students show mastery. For an example of basic, on-level, and advanced task sets for a sixth-grade fractions lesson, look at the differentiated activity examples on page 41. You may want to use the Bloom's Taxonomy List of Activity Options to help you target the appropriate level of challenge.

    If you want to differentiate the assignment by offering tasks that appeal to student strengths, you may want to create a variety of tasks that tap visual-spatial, bodily-kinesthetic, logical-mathematical, and/or other intelligences. For an example of an assignment differentiated by multiple intelligences, see the westward expansion cube on page 42 and the examples of differentiated student products on page 43. You may want to refer to the Multiple Intelligence Menu of Activity Ideas as you create the tasks.

3. Use a copy of the cube template to prepare a draft of each cube. If you are tiering the activity based on readiness, use colored copy paper to make different-

colored cubes for each readiness group. (Depending on the size of your groups, you may need to make more than one of each cube. One cube per every four to five students can be used as a gauge as to how many cubes to construct.)

Think Dots Variation

To vary the cube format and maintain the same differentiation strategy, use the Think Dots format. Write the activities you developed in Step 2 of the procedures on the back of the Think Dots Template cards (page 40) instead of the sides of the cube template. Cut out and laminate the cards for durability. Punch a hole in the upper left corner of the cards and clip them together with an O-ring. Let students draw a number (1–6) or roll a die to determine which task they will do.

---

4. Present the cube(s) to the class. Review directions for each task on the cube. If students are unfamiliar with a task procedure, be sure to model the task first. If possible, provide product examples from each activity listed on the cube.

5. Be sure to explain rules and procedures for completing the activities with the whole class. For example, you may want students to complete one activity individually and, if they have time, work with a partner on a second activity.

6. Have students assess their work with the Cubing Checklist and revise as needed before they hand it in. Both you and your students may use the Cubing Rubric to score their final product.

Bloom's Taxonomy List of Activity Options

Verbs to Stimulate Thinking	Complementary Activities
Level 1: Knowledge	
define, name, record, match, select, underline, cite, sort, list, memorize, relate, show, give an example, label, recall, locate, group, recite, choose, describe	1. Make an acrostic. 2. Describe the _____. 3. Make a timeline of events. 4. Write a list. 5. Match names of people to their time period. 6. Make a chart.
Level 2: Comprehension	
explain, tell, express, summarize, list, identify, calculate, restate, paraphrase, discuss, locate, retell, research, convert, annotate, describe, report, recognize, review, observe, locate, outline	1. Cut out pictures to show an event. 2. Illustrate the main idea. 3. Summarize the procedure. 4. Write a dialogue that describes _____. 5. Outline a chapter. 6. Write a news report. 7. Prepare a flow chart.
Level 3: Application	
apply, manipulate, relate, illustrate, interview, sketch, change, prepare, translate, experiment, compute, show, solve, demonstrate, construct, teach, adapt, interpret, make, produce, sequence	1. Construct a model. 2. Make a display to illustrate one event. 3. Translate a chapter into a one-act play. 4. Design a map to include important information about an event. 5. Demonstrate a procedure for the class/a peer. 6. Solve a problem by two different methods.

Bloom's Taxonomy List of Activity Options (continued)

Verbs to Stimulate Thinking	Complementary Activities
Level 4: Analysis	
classify, solve, arrange, examine, distinguish, contrast, survey, compare, appraise, differentiate, separate, discriminate, question, interpret, analyze, categorize, investigate, organize	1. Design a questionnaire. 2. Conduct an investigation and interpret the data. 3. Construct a graph that compares two or three sets of data. 4. Write a review of a play or book. 5. Review _____ in terms of identified criteria. 6. Prepare a report about the area of study.
Level 5: Synthesis	
compose, infer, develop, forecast, construct, formulate, predict, arrange, propose, compile, generalize, create, design, originate, assemble, predict, suppose, revise	1. Create a model that shows your new ideas. 2. Devise an original experiment to test _____. 3. Finish the incomplete task. 4. Make a hypothesis. 5. Change _____ so that it will _____. 6. Propose a new method to _____. 7. Give the book a more appropriate title.
Level 6: Evaluation	
debate, estimate, prioritize, assess, appraise, support, revise, evaluate, validate, recommend, rank, conclude, judge, determine	1. Prepare a list of criteria for judging _____. Indicate priority ratings you would give. 2. Conduct a debate. 3. Prepare an annotated bibliography. 4. Form a discussion panel. 5. Prepare a case to present your opinions. 6. List some common assumptions and interpret your reactions to these assumptions.

Multiple Intelligences Menu of Activity Ideas

Verbal-Linguistic

Make a commercial.
Write a play, poem, or story.
Make an audiotape.
Conduct an interview.
Organize a debate.
Write directions for _____.

Intrapersonal

Write a diary entry.
Discuss with a peer what you think it would feel
    like to _____.
Compose an op-ed piece: "If I were in _____'s
    shoes, what would I do?"
Explain how you feel about _____.
Support your opinion.
Create a personal goal sheet.
Compare and contrast your response with
    someone else's.

Bodily-Kinesthetic

Make a model.
Role-play a situation.
Play character charades.
Invent a game.
Devise a scavenger hunt.
Choreograph movement.

Logical-Mathematical

Make a web or hierarchical organizer.
Make analogies to explain something.
Make a spreadsheet to show information or data.
Make a timeline.
Categorize the material by key attributes.

Visual-Spatial

Make a bulletin board display.
Create a cartoon strip.
Illustrate a story.
Create a PowerPoint™ presentation or slide show.
Design an advertisement.

Musical-Rhythmic

Compose a song, rap, or rhythmic poem.
Write a commercial jingle.
Choose song titles for _____.
Research sounds specific to _____.

Naturalist

Organize materials into categories.
Describe what you would see in nature during _____.
Show how nature would be affected by _____.
Create an experiment about _____.
How would a _____ (something in nature) respond
    to _____?

Interpersonal

Organize a group outing.
Create a short skit.
Conduct a survey.
Record a conversation.
Organize a debate.
Write a script for a telemarketer.
Give a presentation as a tour guide.

The Cube

Write a task in each square. Cut around the outline and fold in along the dotted lines to create a cube. Put dots of glue on the tabs and attach them inside the cube to secure.

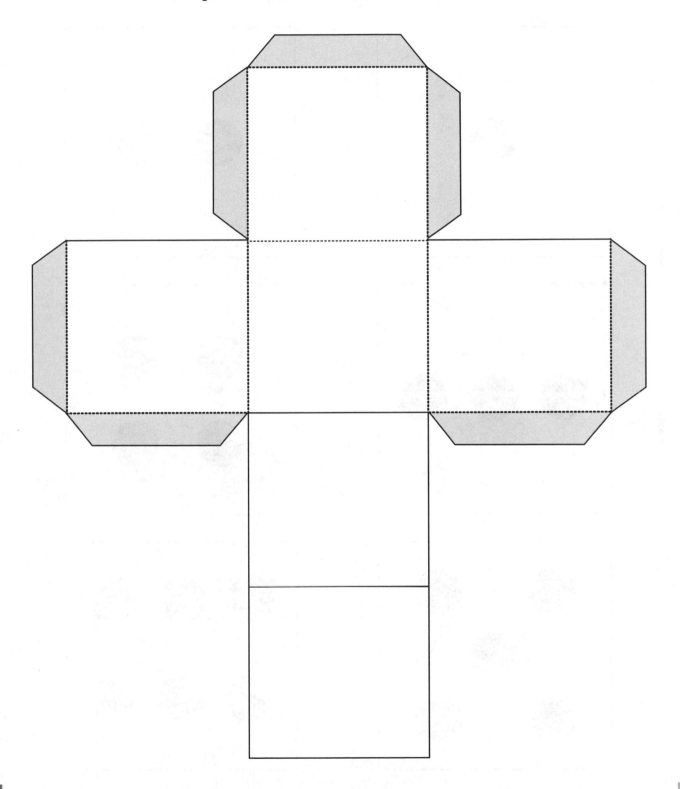

Think Dots

Cut out the cards and write a task on the back of each. Laminate for durability. Punch a hole in the upper left corner of the cards and clip them together with an O-ring.

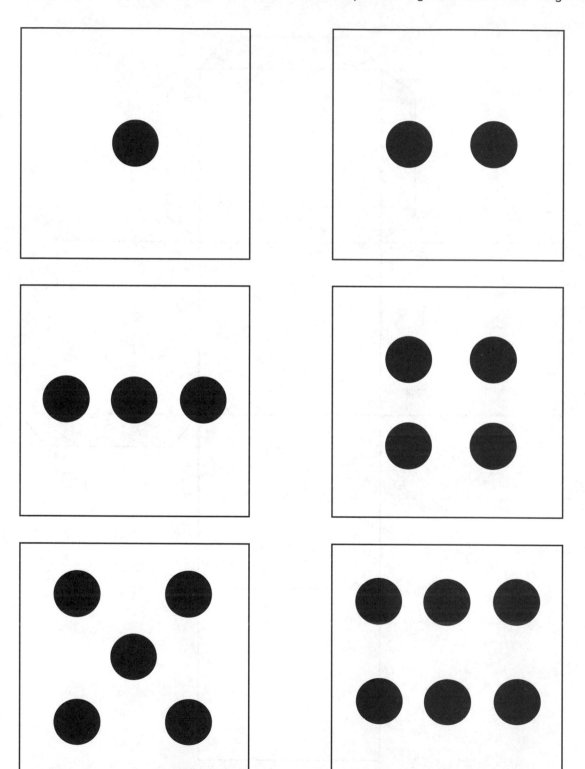

Cubing

Math: Fractions

The cube assignment sets below were created for a multilevel sixth-grade class upon the completion of several lessons on fraction equivalencies. The basic-level cube is designed for students who are working on simple fraction relationships, the on-level cube tasks are suited to students who can perform basic operations with fractions, and the cube with above-level tasks appropriately challenges students who can do more sophisticated operations with fractions. (Note: These assignments require dice, fraction dice, fraction cards, and dominoes.)

Basic-Level Assignment

- Make a list of six equivalent fractions for 5/6.
- Roll one fraction die and decide what you would have to add to the fraction to get a whole. Write the equation.
- Roll one fraction die and draw the fraction using a pie diagram.
- Roll one fraction die and draw the fraction using circles, squares, or rectangles.
- Roll one die and use that number for the denominator. What would the numerator need to be to create a whole?
- Create two fractions that are more than 1/4 and two fractions that are less than 2/5.

On-Level Assignment

- Using three dominoes, place the three fractions in order from smallest to largest.
- Roll two fraction dice and write a number story using the fractions.
- Using four dominoes, record the improper fractions and create mixed numerals.
- Roll a fraction die and draw a pie diagram showing that fraction. List three more equivalent fractions that also represent your pie.
- Roll one blue die for the denominator and two red dice for the numerators. Add and record your equation.
- Choose four fraction cards and place them in order from smallest to largest.

Above-Level Assignment

- Roll two fraction dice. Make up a story problem that includes those two fractions. Solve it.
- Roll one whole die along with a fraction die and convert the mixed numeral into an improper fraction.
- Roll three fraction dice. Add them and draw a picture that represents that number sentence.
- Roll two fraction dice and find a common denominator for them.
- Subtract the larger fraction from the smaller one. Draw a diagram to show your answer.
- Roll a die to get a numerator. Find the denominator that would make the fraction equal to 1/4, 1/6, and 1/2.
- Choose six fraction cards. Put them in order from largest to smallest.

Cubing

Social Studies: Westward Expansion

The cube below was created to gauge students' understanding of westward expansion in America in the 1800s and to differentiate the assignment by learning style. Following several lessons on the Oregon Trail and the Oregon Country, students were asked to roll the cube twice and complete the two activities described. The essential questions in the unit (listed below) and the learning styles of the students in the class both guided the development of the activities.

Essential questions targeted for the cube activity:

• What effect did this expansion have on all people involved?

• What would it be like to live on the frontier or move to a new land?

• What effect did this expansion have on indigenous people who were living in that area?

• How did westward expansion change the culture of the United States?

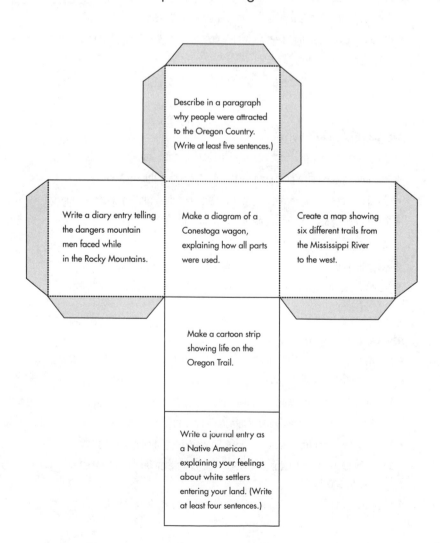

Describe in a paragraph why people were attracted to the Oregon Country. (Write at least five sentences.)

Write a diary entry telling the dangers mountain men faced while in the Rocky Mountains.

Make a diagram of a Conestoga wagon, explaining how all parts were used.

Create a map showing six different trails from the Mississippi River to the west.

Make a cartoon strip showing life on the Oregon Trail.

Write a journal entry as a Native American explaining your feelings about white settlers entering your land. (Write at least four sentences.)

Cubing: Social Studies

(Westward expansion and the Oregon Country assignment, page 42)

ASSIGNMENT NOTES:

The cartoon strip activity incorporated the essential questions "What effect did this expansion have on all people involved?" and "What would it be like to live on the frontier or move to a new land?" This artfully designed example answers both questions in the vernacular of a young pioneer.

This Native American journal entry answers the essential question "What effect did this expansion have on indigenous people who were living in that area?" This student assumed the role of a Native American whose land had been taken from her without consent. The emotionally charged response shows a high level of historical knowledge and the ability to see the perspective of another person.

CUBING CHECKLIST

Name _____ Date _____

Cube activity _____

Accuracy
❑ I've carefully checked the information presented in my activity. It is supported by the text and/or class work.

❑ I need to check the following parts: _____

_____

Completion
❑ I completed the entire activity.

❑ These are steps I still need to complete: _____

_____

Focus
❑ I stuck to the cube activity I rolled. _____

_____

❑ I did some parts differently. (Explain.) _____

_____

Mechanics
❑ For any written parts of the activity, I checked punctuation, spelling, and grammar.

❑ For any mathematical parts of the activity, I've double-checked my calculations and shown my work.

❑ I still need to check the following mechanics: _____

Neatness
❑ The overall quality of this cube activity is the best work I can do.

❑ I could still improve the following: _____

Changes made:
❑

❑

❑

❑

Date turned in: _____

Cubing Rubric

Assignment Traits					
Accuracy The information is correct. It is fully supported by the text and/or class work.	5	4	3	2	1
	Comments:				
Task Completion The task is complete and represents the student's best work.	5	4	3	2	1
	Comments:				
Focus The student stayed focused on the task and fully developed the chosen task with many details and examples.	5	4	3	2	1
	Comments:				
Mechanics The writing contains very few mechanical errors and was checked for punctuation, spelling, and grammar.	5	4	3	2	1
	Comments:				
Neatness The overall quality of this product is very high and is as good as or better than the student's other work.	5	4	3	2	1
	Comments:				

Grade (based on levels attained for each criterion)

Scoring key				Assessment guide
25–24 = A+	19 = B+	14 = C+	10 = D	5 = Advanced
23–21 = A	18–16 = B	13–12 = C	9 = D–	4 = Proficient
20 = A–	15 = B–	11 = C–		3 = Basic
				2 = Below Basic
				1 = Novice

Strategies for Differentiating in the Content Areas © 2007 by Beverly Strayer and Troy Strayer, Scholastic Teaching Resources

CHAPTER 4

Note-Taking Strategies

CONTENT OBJECTIVE:
Reinforce students' understanding of required content-area material through meaningful note-taking strategies.

DIFFERENTIATION APPROACH:
Vary the process by which students learn key information and ideas by incorporating students' interests and learning styles.

In every content area, we deal with information that is best presented to students in a traditional outline. Yet not all students easily grasp information presented in this format. Unless students have strong language skills and can navigate the outline easily, they often find that reviewing their notes is frustrating: once time has lapsed between the presentation of the information in class and the independent work of reviewing, many of the abbreviated notes and new terms have lost their meanings, and relationships among the ideas become cloudy. We have not succeeded in helping students connect with and separate the meaningful ideas from the overwhelming amount of information they take in during the course of the day.

The note-taking strategies included in this chapter provide you with an opportunity to present key information and concepts in a way that students can interact with and connect to. When this happens, students' retention of information increases, their confidence soars, and they have a deeper understanding of the content they've learned.

These note-taking strategies can be differentiated by interest or learning profile. Each strategy invites students to choose how they wish to depict the information in their notes, thus personalizing the task and increasing their interest in the topic. Students may show their notes through words, pictures, or a combination of the two, to create a meaningful resource for learning and reviewing the material.

Note-Taking Strategy 1: Picture Notes

Students enjoy recasting standard notes using their own picture and text codes. They make an illustrated guide to their notes, which serves as an excellent study aid.

Materials

- sheet of paper
- (optional) materials that can draw attention to key ideas and help students with their sketches, such as colored pencils, highlighters, sticky notes, or rulers

Procedure

1. Find a selection from a textbook or part of a lecture you want your students to learn well.

2. Format your paper so that there is a vertical line down the middle of the page.

3. Organize your content in Roman numeral form with as many subheadings as you need on the left side of the page. Leave the right side of the page blank (see example, page 55). You may opt to have students copy the format from an overhead transparency or to give them copies of the notes. (You'll need to use several pages for this technique. Even if your notes can be condensed to one page of standard notes, you may need to create two or more pages in this format to allow plenty of room for students to respond in the right-hand column.)

4. When you present the notes to students, tell them that the right side of the page is where they will make notes with pictures and words that translate the information on the left side of the page into their "own language." Emphasize to students that their notes should include different illustrated responses from those of their peers because their understanding of the content is unique to them.

Reviewing notes: To have students review the material, simply fold the paper on the vertical line and have students explain

We have been using these note-taking strategies for many years in place of the traditional outline format to help students learn about a range of topics—from the colony of Jamestown to the water cycle. These strategies allow our students to take new information and learn it in a way that sticks. This type of note-taking puts students in the driver's seat, making them active participants, rather than passive recorders of information. When they make meaningful associations that help them recall important information, both their independence in learning new material and their confidence increase.

what their pictures mean to a partner, who can check for accuracy by reading the left side of the page. They can quiz themselves by looking at the picture side only, jotting notes about what they remember on a separate sheet, and then comparing the accuracy of their new notes with the original notes. Making meaning of the series of pictures will help students practice connecting the ideas and reinforcing the important information. You can display collected picture notes for a quiz or review them on a smart board or an overhead projector.

Note-Taking Strategy 2: Movie Frame Notes

Students have the option of working from picture to words or words to picture. The movement between picture and words helps reinforce their understanding of the content in two different ways.

A quick conference about the chapter's main ideas with Movie Frame Notes

Materials

- Movie Frame Notes template (page 53)
- (optional) materials listed for Strategy #1

Procedure

1. Find a selection from a textbook or part of a lecture you want your students to learn well.

2. Use the four-frame Movie Frame Notes template or create your own by organizing a sheet of paper into a two-, three-, or four- frame format. How many boxes you include on a page depends on the amount of information you want students to absorb and how many movie frames you want them to draw for the lesson.

3. Distribute copies to students and have them work in one of two ways, depending on their interests and readiness levels: They may first fill in the notes section and then draw a pictorial representation of those notes in the box on the left side of the page (allow them to draw a simple picture or symbol—the level of detail they include may reflect their learning style); or they may first draw the key images and then fill the notes in to explain the pictures. To support struggling learners, you may want to supply the notes on the right side of the page and have them create the pictures only.

Reviewing notes: As with the first strategy, to help students review the material, have them fold the paper vertically between the pictures and the words and quiz one another in pairs. The first partner can read the note side of the page while the second partner views the pictures and explains what his or her pictures mean. As with the first strategy, when students describe the meaning of the series of pictures, they make stronger connections among the ideas. You can display collected picture notes for a quiz or review them on a smart board or an overhead projector.

Note-Taking Strategy 3: Poof Book Notes

The small format of these easy-to-make booklets is much less intimidating than a blank page. Students creatively organize key information on a topic or subtopic you're studying.

Materials

- sheet of paper
- Poof Book Instructions (page 52)
- (optional) materials listed for Strategy #1

Procedure

1. Find a selection from a textbook or part of a lecture you want your students to learn well. Poof Books provide an excellent format for learning about a multistep process, exploring a slice of a complex issue or topic, or examining a topic that has various levels of meaning (see example, page 57).

2. Give each student a sheet of paper and post or distribute copies of Poof Book Instructions. Be sure to model the process for the class. (Once they have completed this process a few times, your students will be able to construct the books with ease. The book itself takes about two minutes to construct and students love to make them.)

3. Use the Poof Books flexibly to gather notes; you might have students use each page for showing part of a whole or a step in a cycle. For example, you might have them title the cover "The Water Cycle" and have them design or put a key word or phrase on each page to show the steps involved. Or when students study the process of how a bill becomes a law, you might have students make diagrams and descriptions of each stage of the process.

Reviewing notes: Students will enjoy rereading their handmade notebook in a page-by-page fashion, much like a story—because only a small amount of information can fit on a page, this makes for quick, easy reading. You might also challenge students to open to one page of the book and quiz themselves on what comes before and after that step or piece of information.

Note-Taking Strategy 4: Three-Column Notes

This strategy is built on repeated exposure to the same notes. Students work from part to whole and then whole to part as they fill in details, then subtopics, and topics in three versions of the same outline.

Materials

- word-processing program
- (optional) materials listed for Strategy #1

Procedure

1. Find a selection from a textbook or part of a lecture you want your students to learn well.

2. Create a table in a document so that you divide your paper into three equal columns.

3. In the first column, create a blank outline that represents the main ideas and details from the material you've selected. The outline should include spaces for the topics (marked by Roman numerals), subtopics (marked by letters) and supporting details (marked by numbers). Type in the information for the topics only, leaving the subtopics and details blank for the students to fill in.

4. In the second column, paste in the blank outline, and type in only the information for the subtopics, leaving the topics and details blank for students to fill in.

I. Skeletal System
A.
1.
2.
B.
1.
2.
C.
1.
2.
D.
1.
2.
E.
1.
2.

5. In the third column, once again paste in the blank outline, and type in only the information for the details, leaving the topics and subtopics blank for students to fill in (see example, page 54).

6. Distribute copies of your notes page to students and have them fold the page in thirds so they are looking at only the left-hand column. As students read the material or listen to the lecture, have them fill in the subtopics and details in this column. After the reading or lecture (in class or at home), have them complete the remaining columns to review each subtopic and detail along the way. Challenge students to keep their paper folded so that they cannot see the other sections and then cross-check their work.

Reviewing notes: Make a blank overhead of either of the three columns and have students work with a partner or within a flexible group to fill it in. This gives them the opportunity to fill in the pieces of the meaning puzzle in several different ways and have peers coach each other where there are gaps in understanding.

Poof Book Instructions

1. Fold an 8.5 x 11 inch sheet of paper in half vertically (hot-dog style) and crease the fold. Unfold.

2. Fold the paper in half horizontally (hamburger style) and crease the fold. Leave it folded.

3. Fold the paper in half again vertically and crease the fold. Unfold this last step.

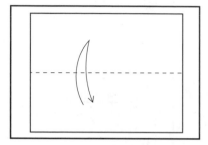

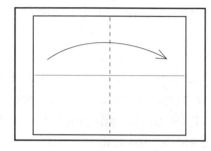

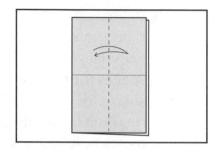

4. At the horizontal crease, carefully cut or tear at the center of the folded edge until you reach the midway point.

5. Open up the paper again and you will see a slit in the middle of the paper.

6. Fold the paper again like a hot dog so the tear is at the top of the paper.

7. Hold each end of the paper and push your hands together, opening the tear. Bring your hands together until the paper takes the shape of a large addition sign.

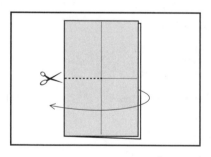

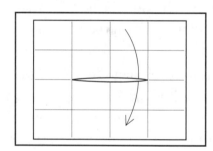

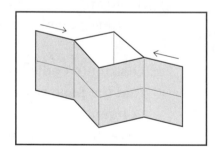

8. Push all the sections together until you have an eight-page book.

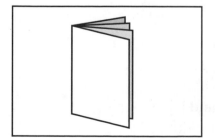

Movie Frame Notes

Three-Column Notes

Science: Anatomy

In an eighth-grade health lesson, students used this three-column format to organize and review key information about the skeletal system. Students folded this page into thirds and filled in the left-hand column during the mini-lecture, then the middle column as a closure activity at the end of the lesson. At the beginning of class the next day, the teacher showed the right-hand column and the students worked in pairs to recall the information and fill in the subtopics.

Skeletal System Three-Column Notes

I. Skeletal System	I. Skeletal System	I. Skeletal System
A.	**A.** Allow Movement 1. 2.	**A.** _____ 1. points of attachment for muscles 2. these points move when muscles pull on bones
B.	**B.** Provide Support 1. 2.	**B.** _____ 1. backbone (vertebrae) 2. support your head, spinal cord and upper body
C.	**C.** Protection 1. 2.	**C.** _____ 1. provides protection for organs 2. ex. ribs protect heart and lungs
D.	**D.** Form New Blood Cells 1. 2.	**D.** _____ 1. marrow – tissue in center of some bones 2. helps to form red and white blood cells
E.	**E.** Store Minerals 1. 2.	**E.** _____ 1. storage centers for minerals 2. ex. Calcium and Phosphorous

Picture Notes: Social Studies

(American History, Response to French Revolution)

ASSIGNMENT NOTES:

This example shows one student's notes in two parts: the outline notes she copied from the board as the class discussed George Washington's foreign policy and the pictures she drew on the right-hand side to personalize those notes. To review, she and her classmates were asked to fold their picture notes in half and, looking at the picture side only, summarize their notes for their table partners, who, in turn, checked these responses on the side with the written notes.

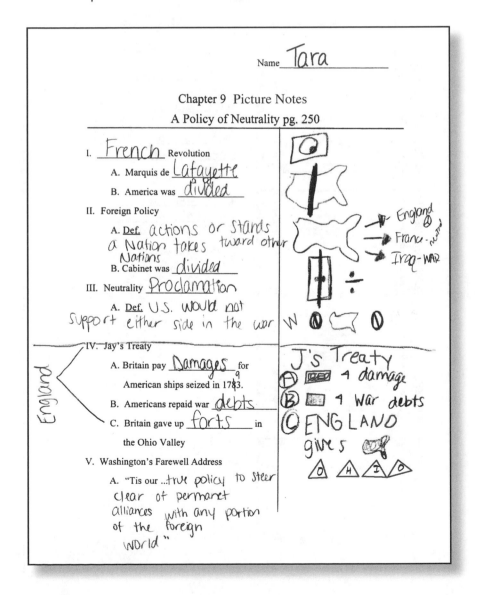

Name Tara

Chapter 9   Picture Notes
A Policy of Neutrality pg. 250

I. French Revolution
   A. Marquis de Lafayette
   B. America was divided

II. Foreign Policy
   A. Def. actions or stands a Nation takes toward other Nations
   B. Cabinet was divided

III. Neutrality Proclamation
   A. Def. U.S. would not support either side in the war

IV. Jay's Treaty
   A. Britain pay Damages for American ships seized in 1783.
   B. Americans repaid war debts
   C. Britain gave up forts in the Ohio Valley

V. Washington's Farewell Address
   A. "Tis our ...true policy to steer clear of permanet alliances with any portion of the foreign world"

Movie Frame Notes: Science

(Biology, the Water Cycle)

ASSIGNMENT NOTES:

An eighth-grade earth science student used movie frame notes to organize information about the water cycle, shown here in four steps. The teacher provided the information for students to fill in beside each frame and then asked students to draw a picture that would correspond with the written words. At the conclusion of the lesson, students engaged in an A–B Conversation (page 94) to summarize the lesson in terms they would remember.

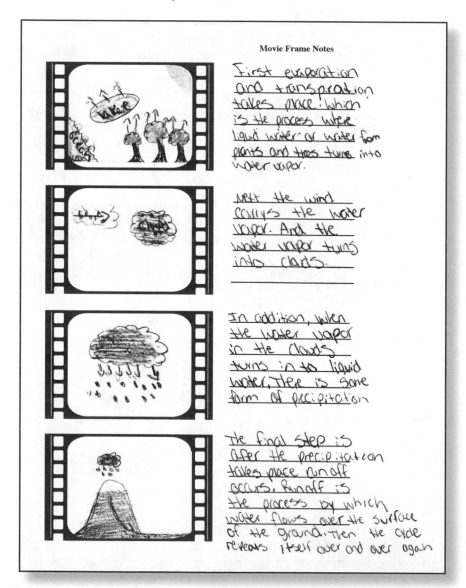

Movie Frame Notes

First evaporation and transpration takes place; which is the process where liquid water or water from plants and trees turns into water vapor.

Next the wind carrys the water vapor. And the water vapor turns into clouds.

In addition, when the water vapor in the clouds turns in to liquid water, There is some form of precipitation

The final step is after the precipitation takes place run off occurs. Runoff is the process by which water flows over the surface of the ground. Then the cycle repeats itself over and over again

Poof Book Notes: Family and Consumer Science

ASSIGNMENT NOTES:

When introducing students to different types of fabrics in an eighth-grade family and consumer science class, the teacher used a multi-sensory approach, providing actual fabric samples with a mini-lecture. She had students create a Poof Book to show and describe the samples. Here, a student has named the fabric on the top of each page, written a short description of the fabric, and then stapled a piece of that fabric to the page.

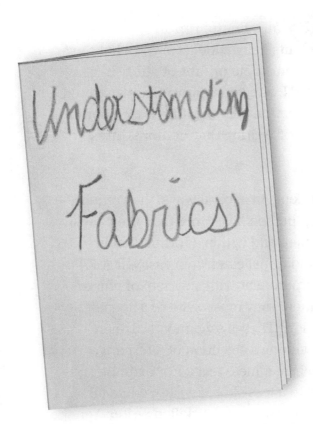

CHAPTER 5

R.A.F.T.-ing (Role, Audience, Format, Topic)

CONTENT OBJECTIVE:
Students demonstrate in detail what they know about a specific topic

DIFFERENTIATION APPROACH:
Vary the products students create by tapping into their interests and learning preferences (students choose audience, format, and voice for their writing assignment)

A welcome alternative to worksheets, reports, projects, or tests, R.A.F.T. assignments help students show what they have learned about a current topic or unit of study in a creative, choice-based format. R.A.F.T. assignments are also structured to help students organize the information they've gathered, elaborate on it, and create a coherent piece of writing that demonstrates their understanding.

R.A.F.T. assignments motivate students in several ways: they require students to write on a topic from a perspective other than their own, to an audience that is not the teacher, and within a format that is usually more engaging than the traditional classroom essay. R.A.F.T.-ing also encourages students to experiment with a variety of voices in their writing; with each assignment they must write to a specific audience from a unique point of view. These assignments also encourage students to choose from among a selection of alternative writing formats that best meet their readiness level. For example, a TV commercial script may appeal to a less-skilled writer, while an op-ed article may appropriately challenge a more skilled writer. Yet both students will work with the information at the synthesis level of Bloom's Taxonomy.

A R.A.F.T. assignment may be used as a formative assessment during a unit of study or as a summative assessment at the end of a unit of study. Using it as an assessment tool can help you determine whether students understand the topic well or need more instruction. The checklist and rubric at the end of this chapter may be used to assess any R.A.F.T. product.

R.A.F.T. Elements

R—Role of the Writer: Students may choose to write from a variety of perspectives which range from the familiar (they may write from their own point of view) to the unfamiliar (they may take on the persona of a rapper, falcon, soldier, heart, reporter, or scientist). Writing from different points of view helps students develop critical thinking skills.

A—Audience: Students often enjoy writing for audiences other than their teacher. Audience options for a R.A.F.T. assignment may include friends, a future employer, or a historical figure. Selecting and writing to a specific audience requires students to use the appropriate language and style needed to convey meaning. This is a great opportunity to review differences in tone and style (formal or informal) and teach students how to address different audiences appropriately.

F—Format: Students have the opportunity to try out "real life" writing formats, such as speeches, want ads, songs, or persuasive letters. Experimenting with format allows students to gain control of writing forms other than the traditional school essay; choosing the format is also a strong motivator, especially for struggling writers.

T—Topic: This is the subject of the writing. You may choose the topic or allow students to choose from several subtopics that cover a central topic. You'll want to help students ensure that the role and audience selected are appropriate for the topic and relevant to the content.

Materials

- Verbs for R.A.F.T. Assignments (page 62)
- R.A.F.T. Formats (page 63)
- R.A.F.T. Checklist (page 68)
- R.A.F.T. Rubric (page 69)

The R.A.F.T. approach was introduced to us five years ago at a district workshop on differentiated instruction, and we have been using R.A.F.T. assignments successfully in our classrooms ever since. We get especially good results when we offer them as a summative assessment option. The format allows students who do not do well on pencil and paper tests to show their understanding in a way that is comfortable as well as creative for them. Most students put more time, energy, and enthusiasm into preparing a R.A.F.T. assignment than studying for any test we could design.

Procedure

1. Select the objective on which you want to focus. To determine how much structure to add to the R.A.F.T. assignment, evaluate students' readiness. Introduce the R.A.F.T. assignment format to the class or review it with them, explaining that all writers must consider not only their topic, but also their audience and the form their writing will take. Knowing these parameters will help them develop a plan of action. Tell students that their writing will reflect the elements of *role*, *audience*, *format*, and *topic*. Be sure to review each element with them, starting with the topic and giving examples as shown below. (As a reference for students, you might use a transparency or poster like the one shown here.)

R.A.F.T. It!

R = Role
Who are you, the writer?

A = Audience
Who will read your writing?

F = Format
How will you present your ideas and information? What's your purpose?

T = Topic
What is the writing about?

Role: Who are you, the writer? Are you Abraham Lincoln? A cell? The heart? Oxygen?
 • Encourage students to think creatively: Who or what would best describe or present this topic?

Audience: Who will be reading this writing? A friend? The nucleus? The lungs?
 • Make sure students understand that the audience must make sense in the context of the topic and role they choose.

Format: How will you present the information? A letter? An ad? A song? A poem? What is your purpose in presenting the topic you've selected? Is it to persuade? to call for action? to educate someone? Does the format match the purpose?
 • Be sure to offer students a choice of formats with which they are already familiar and comfortable or add and model a new format. See the R.A.F.T. Format List for options. If this is the first time students have done a R.A.F.T. assignment, give them only two, three, or four format choices, so that they are not overwhelmed.
 • The R.A.F.T. Verbs list gives students a choice of words to help them state their purpose.

Topic: What is the subject of your writing?
  • You may want to provide the topic or give students a list of related topics from which to choose.

3. Have students fill in a four-column prewriting chart like the one below to organize their ideas before they write. Depending on their level of independence, you may want to fill in one or more of the elements to help structure their work. We find that adding a strong verb stating the purpose of the writing in the format section helps students better focus their writing. (See the R.A.F.T. Prewriting Charts on pages 64–65.)

Role	Audience	Format (and Purpose)	Topic

4. On the board or overhead, demonstrate, model, and think aloud how students might complete a R.A.F.T. assignment, starting with the prewriting chart in Step 3 (above) and moving through the writing process.

5. Share with students the R.A.F.T.-ing Rubric or your own assignment criteria list so they are familiar with your expectations for the assignment.

6. For scaffolded practice, assign students to small, heterogeneous groups to write a short piece based on a R.A.F.T. prewriting chart you've provided. Have groups share their completed R.A.F.T.s with the class. Once students feel comfortable with the process, assign a new R.A.F.T. or let students create their own for independent work. Provide students with as many choices as they can handle.

7. Have students evaluate a first draft of their work using the R.A.F.T.-ing Checklist and then revise as needed before they turn the finished piece in to you. They may self-assess using the R.A.F.T.-ing Rubric, or you may use this rubric to score their final piece.

Verbs for R.A.F.T. Assignments

analyze	explain
announce	illustrate
apply	inform
characterize	interview
clarify	investigate
combine	persuade
communicate	quote
compare	record
construct	reflect
contrast	relate
create	review
critique	rhyme
describe	script
design	sell
draw	summarize
encourage	warn

R.A.F.T. Formats

Advertisement	Last Will and Testament
Announcement	Letter
Board Game	List
Brochure	Math Word Problem/Solution
Children's Book	Memo
Comic Strip	Menu
Comparison Paragraph	Monologue
Conversation	Myth
Debate	News Story
Diary	Persuasive Letter
Directions for "How To"	Play
Editorial	Poems
E-mail	Raps
Epitaph	Resume
Eulogy	Script
Fairy Tale	Songs
Five Paragraph Essay	Story Board
Greeting Card	Telegram
Instructions	Test
Interview	Timeline
Job Description	"Wanted" Poster
Journal Entry	Word Puzzle & Games

R.A.F.T. Prewriting Charts

Science: Rain Forest

This Rain Forest R.A.F.T. chart offers students four or five teacher-created choices as well as an option to create their own. We have found that as creative as we think we are in writing the R.A.F.T. choices, students always come up with great ideas. Their R.A.F.T.s often become one of our assignment choices the next year.

Role	Audience	Format (purpose)	Topic
Environmentalist	Senator	Speech (call to action)	Protect the Rain Forest
Tree	Animals	Advertisement (encourage)	Rooms for rent
Travel Agent	Traveler	Brochure (summarize)	Why visit the Rain Forest?
Canopy	Understory	Song (entertain)	We belong together
Student Choice	Student Choice	Student Choice	Student Choice

Math: Fractions

In preparation for our state math assessment, we incorporate lots of writing into our math lessons. The R.A.F.T. choices we developed for our fractions unit provide a unique, motivating way to have students demonstrate their understanding of fractions through writing.

Role	Audience	Format (purpose)	Topic
Improper Fraction	Mixed Number	Poem (summarize)	Sometimes it's okay to be improper
Fraction	Whole Number	Song (entertain)	I need to be reduced
Decimal	Fraction	Letter (thank-you note)	Thank you for supporting me
Denominator	Numerator	Rap (entertain)	You can't have one without the other
Student Choice	Student Choice	Student Choice	Student Choice

Social Studies: Westward Expansion

Westward expansion is an interesting topic for many eighth graders and they enjoy putting themselves into the era. Many have seen Westerns on TV and have misconceptions about the people of the era. A R.A.F.T. assignment allows the students to demonstrate their knowledge of the era in an exciting, challenging way.

Role	Audience	Format (purpose)	Topic
A Texan	Santa Anna	Treaty (comprehend)	The need to give Texas its independence
A forty-niner	Family	Journal (inform)	All the sights and people you meet in the California Gold Rush
Native American	Pioneers	Song lyric (entertain)	The need to live together in the west and share the land
Slave	President of the U.S.	Business letter (persuade)	The need to not allow slavery to expand west
Student Choice	Student Choice	Student Choice	Student Choice

Reading: *Where the Red Fern Grows*

Where the Red Fern Grows is a favorite read-aloud of fifth- and sixth-grade boys who grow up in a rural area. Many are hunters and own hunting dogs. The main character, Billy, is someone with whom they can connect. This particular book has "hooked" many of my reluctant readers. When it comes time to demonstrate their understanding of the book, they love the R.A.F.T. activities. Many basic readers produce amazing writing based on the R.A.F.T. suggestions.

Role	Audience	Format (purpose)	Topic
Grandpa	Billy	Letter (encourage)	Winning the contest
Little Ann	Old Dan	Song (entertain)	My big brother
Raccoon	Old Dan	Poem (write creatively)	I'm smarter than you'll ever be
Billy	Little Ann	Sonnet (empathize)	Please don't go
Student Choice	Student Choice	Student Choice	Student Choice

R.A.F.T.: Math

(Fractions assignment, page 64)

ASSIGNMENT NOTES:

For many of our math students, explaining mathematical relationships can be a challenge. For this assignment, the R.A.F.T. choices we offered gave students a way to explain the relationship between parts of a fraction in an accessible way. The student who completed the assignment below loved to write poetry and sing but detested writing paragraphs. With a differentiated assignment, he was able to demonstrate his understanding of the parts of a fraction through a rap about two inseparable brothers, delivered in the voice of a denominator talking to his little brother, the numerator. He chose the following assignment:

Role: Denominator
Audience: Numerator
Format: Rap
Topic: You can't have one without the other

Denominator Blues

I am the denominator.
It *is* true.
The bottom number of a fraction,
I'm the whole—and "true blue."

Numerator, you're on the top.
You're just a part of me, little brother.
Because you can't have one
Without the other.

Without either one of us
There *is* no fraction.
It takes both of us
To have fraction action.

I am the denominator.
Numerator, you're my brother.
Remember, you can't have one
Without the other.

R.A.F.T.: Social Studies

(Westward expansion assignment, page 65)

ASSIGNMENT NOTES:

This R.A.F.T. example was created during a unit on westward expansion (page 65). The student demonstrated a solid understanding of the experiences of a forty-niner in a journal entry about her fictional journey. Her writing discusses the myths of the Gold Rush, which lured people to California, the hardships people faced once there, and her meeting John Sutter. The date she chose—one year after the initial rush—informs her description of the hardships she faced while in California.

Role: Forty-niner
Audience: Family
Format: Journal (inform)
Topic: All the sights and people you meet in the California Gold Rush

R.A.F.T   Brittany

Dear Journal,   August 21, 1850

I plan on sending this off to my family so they can read what life has been like for me lately. So, Dear Family, life has been a whirlwind lately. Ever since I left home with you in Boston, I've been wondering if I will live here forever. To tell you the truth, dear family, the gold rush here in California isn't what it is said to be. When we all first heard about gold in California, about two years ago, the newspapers told us that there were streams paved with gold, and gold nuggets scattered loose on the ground. They said we could just start digging - it didn't even take any hard work. We could all make a fortune. But family, that is not so. Here in California, the gold is all but gone. So many miners rushed out here only to find that the best gold was already taken. What's left is far into the ground and takes back breaking labor to find. I'm hungry, family, because the soil here is rocky and the climate is hot. More like a desert, if you ask me! We can't farm enough food to live on. I've met a girl, by the way. Francesca Northington, her name. She's from Boston as well. We plan to move back with you, dear family, As soon as we get rich, that is... if we do! I also met the man who discovered the gold, John Sutter. Quite a man he was! And arrogant as well! Acts like he is king of the world because he found gold in California. haha. What an idea. Well family, seeing as things aren't going well here, I plan on seeing you soon!
        Yours truly,
        John Culpepper Jones

R.A.F.T. CHECKLIST

Name _____ Date _____

R.A.F.T. Activity _____

Accuracy

❑ I've carefully checked the information presented in my activity. It is correct and backed up by research, if needed.

❑ I need to check the following parts: _____

_____

Perspective

❑ I stayed in the chosen role throughout my writing.

❑ These are places where I could make my voice sound more like that person or thing:

_____

_____

Focus

❑ I stuck to the activity described in the directions and developed it fully. _____

_____

❑ I did some parts differently. (Explain.) _____

_____

Mechanics

❑ I've checked punctuation, spelling, and grammar.

❑ I still need to check the following mechanics: _____

Neatness

❑ The overall quality of this writing is the best work I can do.

❑ I could still improve the following: _____

_____

Changes made:

❑

❑

❑

❑

Date turned in: _____

Strategies for Differentiating in the Content Areas © 2007 by Beverly Strayer and Troy Strayer, Scholastic Teaching Resources page 68

R.A.F.T. Rubric

Assignment Traits	←				
Accuracy Is the information correct? Is it fully supported by the text and/or research?	5	4	3	2	1
	Comments:				
Perspective Did the writer stay in the role effectively? Did the voice sound like that of the chosen role (person or thing)?	5	4	3	2	1
	Comments:				
Focus Did the writer stick to the chosen format? Did he or she fully develop the chosen topic with many details and examples?	5	4	3	2	1
	Comments:				
Mechanics Does the writing contain very few mechanical errors? Did the student check punctuation, spelling, and grammar?	5	4	3	2	1
	Comments:				
Benchmark How does the overall quality of this R.A.F.T. compare with the student's other writing? Is this his or her best work?	5	4	3	2	1
	Comments:				

Grade (based on levels attained for each criterion)

Scoring key				Assessment guide
25–24 = A+	19 = B+	14 = C+	10 = D	5 = Advanced
23–21 = A	18–16 = B	13–12 = C	9 = D–	4 = Proficient
20 = A–	15 = B–	11 = C–		3 = Basic
				2 = Below Basic
				1 = Novice

Name _____

Date _____

Strategies for Differentiating in the Content Areas © 2007 by Beverly Strayer and Troy Strayer, Scholastic Teaching Resources

CHAPTER 6

Working With Choice Boards

CONTENT OBJECTIVE:

At the end of a unit of study, students demonstrate mastery of one or more objectives in three ways.

DIFFERENTIATION APPROACH:

Vary the products students create and the content they respond to by tapping their interests and learning preferences (students choose three activities to complete).

Choice boards (also called Tic-Tac-Toe Boards) provide a multi-dimensional way for students to demonstrate what they have learned during a unit of study. In place of a written exam, students complete three projects of their choice based on the unit objectives. Students choose their performance outcomes, thereby taking ownership of the content-area subject matter.

Choice boards are extremely flexible differentiation tools. The format, a grid with spaces for nine activity choices, gives you the option of designing differentiated assignments based on readiness or student interest. For example, as with the cubing strategy in Chapter 3, you may create sets of activities at two or more different levels. Students who are at the knowledge/comprehension/ application level might receive one choice board while students at the analysis/synthesis/evaluation level would receive another set. Copying the boards onto different-colored paper is an easy way to distinguish the tiers.

You may also want to create a choice board with activities based on multiple intelligences or learning styles. In this case, you could make sure that the activity set represents a variety of tasks that appeal to the types of learners in your class. Students then choose those activities with which they feel most comfortable.

The products you ask students to create can range from simple (a bullet-point list) to complex (a Web page plan). You can find a long list of product ideas on page 73. As you brainstorm, you might also want to refer to the lists of activity options organized by Bloom's Taxonomy and multiple intelligences from Chapter 3 (pages 36–38).

Materials

- Performance Product Choices (page 73)
- Choice Board template (page 74)
- Choice Board Checklist (page 78)
- Choice Board Rubric (page 79)

Procedure

1. Use the objective you want your students to demonstrate to help you design nine different tasks based on readiness, multiple intelligences, or learning styles. Also determine how you'll assess the finished work (mid-unit assignment, summative assessment, and so on). For example, as you complete a unit on Texas's independence from Mexico, you might design an end-of-unit assessment in which students complete a set of choice-board activities to show their understanding of the Texans' desire for independence from Mexico and how the siege of the Alamo figured in the struggle for independence (see the assignment example on page 75). A student who enjoys visual artwork and writing might choose to create a model of the Alamo, an acrostic poem about the Lone Star State, and a timeline of events representing the siege of the Alamo.

2. Arrange your choice board according to your purpose for developing it. For a board based on multiple intelligences, you may have an activity for each type of intelligence or your activity set may reflect only two or three intelligences (in this case, the top row may contain activities from the logical-mathematical intelligence, while the middle and bottom rows contain activities from the musical-rhythmic and visual-spatial intelligences respectively). You may want to include one activity that students are required to complete in the center box on the board.

We have been using choice boards since they were introduced to us in 2004 at the National Conference for Differentiated Instruction in Las Vegas. We love the adaptable format and the well-rounded assessment that three tasks provide for each student. Students love having some choice in how they demonstrate mastery of unit objectives. Choice is a big motivator—students tend to be much more creative, thorough, and neat in their approach to the self-selected products than with those that are teacher-selected.

4. Determine how you will allow students to choose their activities. Typically, students choose three choice board activities to complete, but you may want to guide them in their selection. For example, you may set up the activities on the board in a specific way. Will you ask students to complete three activities, vertically, horizontally, or diagonally? Will you allow them to choose any three activities on the board regardless of placement on the board? Will one or two of the activities be required?

5. Explain each choice-board activity and model how to complete it. If you have examples of the completed tasks available, show them to students and encourage them to use these as a point of reference.

6. Be clear about your expectations, establishing a timeline for completing the tasks, criteria for student accountability, and an assessment goal.

7. Have students check their work with the Choice Board Checklist and revise them as needed.

8. To make grading more manageable, you may want to have students make a short presentation of all their products to the class and then select their single best product for a grade. In this way, you can check that all products are complete, but score only one for each student. Use the Choice Board Rubric to score their final products.

Performance Product Choices

Acrostic poem	Flannel board story	Playbill/show program
Advertisement	Flow chart	Poster
Annotated bibliography	Haiku	Puppet show
Awards ceremony	Historical monologue	Quilt
Ballad	Illustration	Radio show
Banner	Informative Essay	Rap
Bar graph	Interpretive dance	Readers Theater
Billboard	Interview	Recycled-material construction
Board game	Invention	
Book jacket	Itinerary	Research paper
Book review	Journal entry	Roundtable discussion
Brochure	Lecture	Simulation
Bulletin board	Letter	Skit
Card game	Line graph	Slide show with PowerPoint™
Cartoon	List	
Clay sculpture	Map	Song
Coat of arms	Mobile	Speech
Collage	Mock trial	Storyboard
Comedy sketch	Model	Storytelling
Comic strip	Mosaic	Thank-you note
Commemorative plaque	Mural	Time capsule
Commemorative stamp	Newspaper article	Timeline
Commentary	One-act play	Topographical map
Commercial	Op-ed piece	Tree chart
Costume show	Oral report	TV broadcast
Debate	Overhead transparency	TV game show
Demonstration	Panel	TV talk show
Diagram	Pantomime	Venn diagram
Diary	Persuasive essay	Video
Diorama	Persuasive speech	Wall hanging
Dramatization	Photographic essay	Web page
Editorial cartoon	Pie chart	Written report
Etching	Play	

Choice Board

Choice Boards

Social Studies: Texas Independence (interest-based)

The activities in this choice board were designed using multiple intelligences to motivate students to show their fullest understanding of the history of Texas and its struggle for independence. Each student was required to complete three activities from the choice board and, prior to turning in each activity, perform a self-assessment to ensure that all requirements were met.

Create an acrostic poem using the term *Lone Star State*. Describe important events in Texas's struggle for independence.	Make a cause/effect chart to show five events that led to the Texans' fighting Mexico for independence.	Create a model of the Alamo using recycled materials. Label the model using sticky-note flags.
Make a time-line of events representing each day of the siege at the Alamo.	Create a storyboard for a documentary about a Texan who helped in the struggle for independence.	Assume the role of a newspaper reporter and report back to Red Lion about the events of Gonzalez, Goliad, and San Jacinto.
Construct a mind map showing four problems the Republic of Texas faced when it was founded.	Write a play showing the last two days of the siege at the Alamo.	"Remember the Alamo" was a battle cry that rallied the Texans to victory. Create a slogan that would motivate our soldiers to keep fighting in Iraq. Summarize why you chose this slogan.

Social Studies: Manifest Destiny (interest-based)

Following a lesson on Manifest Destiny and the impact of this belief on westward expansion, students were required to complete three activities from this Choice Board. These activities were designed using multiple intelligences and the students had choice as to which three assignments they completed.

Create a commercial jingle about Manifest Destiny.	Make a mnemonic to help your classmates remember the meaning of Manifest Destiny.	Create a chart showing migration patterns to the western United States from 1840 to 1850.
Make a word art design that shows the meaning of Manifest Destiny.	Present a definition of Manifest Destiny in a unique way.	Provide a motivational speech convincing Americans that Manifest Destiny is a good thing.
Write a diary entry explaining why you're moving west and why you believe or don't believe in Manifest Destiny.	Create a charade "act" that explains the meaning of Manifest Destiny.	Complete the A-B-C nature hunt for things you would see as you traveled west.

Choice Boards

Language Arts: Reading Response (interest-based)

This language arts choice board provides choices from five of the multiple intelligences: logical-mathematical (Venn diagram), interpersonal (commercial and Readers Theater), musical-rhythmic (poem, song, or rap) visual- spatial (illustrated time line), and verbal-linguistic (paragraph and chapter titles).

Create a Venn diagram showing at least ten ways that two of the main characters in your story think and act differently.	Write and act out a 60-second commercial telling people why they must read your book.	Write a paragraph of six or more sentences that identifies the rising action, climax, and resolution of the book you read.
Make a timeline showing the main events in your book. Include at least 12 events.	You may create an activity of your own, but make sure to get my approval before beginning.	Write new chapter titles for each chapter of your book. After each title, write a brief description why your title choices are good ones.
What was the author's purpose for writing this book? Write a seven-sentence paragraph telling why you believe the author wrote this book.	Write a script for the most important scene in your book. Get friends to help you do a Readers Theater presentation for the whole class.	Write a song, poem, or rap describing the character traits of the main character of your book. Be prepared to share your product with the class.

Biology: Cells (readiness-based)

This Choice Board was organized with knowledge-level tasks as well as synthesis and evaluation choices. We nudge students who are ready for more challenging assignments toward the higher-level thinking choices while encouraging students who are still mastering the content basics to stretch as far as they can (when given a choice, our struggling students often amaze us with their creativity and critical thinking). We require each student to complete two or three choices.

Draw and label the major parts of both a plant and animal cell. (Knowledge)	Use a Venn diagram to compare and contrast plant and animal cells. (Analysis)	You may write your own task here, but please show it to me for approval before beginning the work.
Write a song, poem, or rap that describes why cells are important to all of us. Be prepared to perform it for the class. (Comprehension)	Complete the experiment on page 31 in your textbook. Everyone must do this one. (Analysis)	Assume the role of a TV news reporter and write a script for your show. Explain how yeasts and molds are used in everyday life. (Application)
Create a mind map that shows the various kinds of fungi and their uses. (Application)	State three to five reasons why fungi are important to the production of medicines. (Evaluation)	Fungi need moisture and warmth to grow. Use this information to develop a plan to prevent the growth of mold and mildew in your home. (Synthesis)

Choice Board

(Texas Independence assignment, page 75)

ASSIGNMENT NOTES:

From the Choice Board on Texas Independence (page 75), this student chose to complete the acrostic dealing with important events in the history of Texas and a mind map showing problems faced in its infancy as a republic. In the acrostic, Kayla demonstrated in-depth knowledge of events that lead to Texas's independence. In her mind map, she clearly identified four major problems Texans faced after Texas became a republic. Her pictures add clarity to her words as she expresses the written information in her own way.

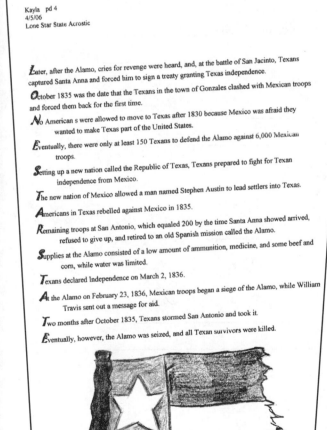

Kayla pd 4
4/5/06
Lone Star State Acrostic

Later, after the Alamo, cries for revenge were heard, and, at the battle of San Jacinto, Texans captured Santa Anna and forced him to sign a treaty granting Texas independence.

October 1835 was the date that the Texans in the town of Gonzales clashed with Mexican troops and forced them back for the first time.

No American s were allowed to move to Texas after 1830 because Mexico was afraid they wanted to make Texas part of the United States.

Eventually, there were only at least 150 Texans to defend the Alamo against 6,000 Mexican troops.

Setting up a new nation called the Republic of Texas, Texans prepared to fight for Texan independence from Mexico.

The new nation of Mexico allowed a man named Stephen Austin to lead settlers into Texas.

Americans in Texas rebelled against Mexico in 1835.

Remaining troops at San Antonio, which equaled 200 by the time Santa Anna showed arrived, refused to give up, and retired to an old Spanish mission called the Alamo.

Supplies at the Alamo consisted of a low amount of ammunition, medicine, and some beef and corn, while water was limited.

Texans declared Independence on March 2, 1836.

At the Alamo on February 23, 1836, Mexican troops began a siege of the Alamo, while William Travis sent out a message for aid.

Two months after October 1835, Texans stormed San Antonio and took it.

Eventually, however, the Alamo was seized, and all Texan survivors were killed.

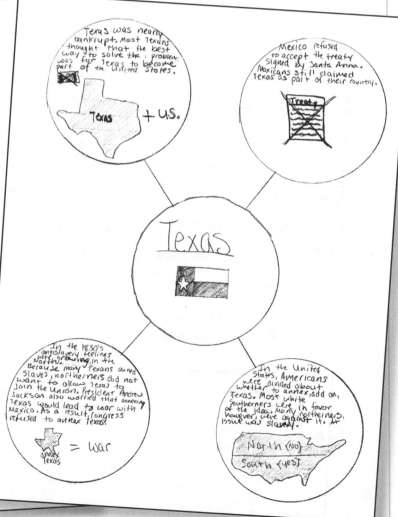

CHOICE BOARD CHECKLIST

Name _____ Date _____

Choice Board Activity _____

Accuracy

❏ I've included all the required elements for each project.

❏ I need to check the following parts: _____

_____

Completion

❏ I completed three choice board activities.

❏ These are parts I still need to complete: _____

_____

Focus

❏ I stuck to the activity described in the directions and developed it fully. _____

_____

❏ I did some parts differently. (Explain.) _____

_____

_____

Mechanics

❏ I've checked punctuation, spelling, and grammar.

❏ I still need to check the following mechanics: _____

Neatness

❏ The overall quality of this writing is the best work I can do.

❏ I could still improve the following: _____

_____

_____

Changes made:

❏

❏

❏

❏   Date turned in: _____

Choice Board Rubric

Name _____

Assignment Traits	←				
Accuracy Is the information included in the finished products accurate?	5	4	3	2	1
	Comments:				
Completion Did the student complete three activities? Are any parts missing?	5	4	3	2	1
	Comments:				
Focus Did the student stick to the activities described in the directions? Did he or she fully develop the chosen activity with many details and examples?	5	4	3	2	1
	Comments:				
Mechanics Does the writing contain very few mechanical errors? Did the student check punctuation, spelling, and grammar?	5	4	3	2	1
	Comments:				
Benchmark How does the overall quality of this assignment compare with the student's other work? Is this his or her best work?	5	4	3	2	1
	Comments:				

Grade (based on levels attained for each criterion)

Scoring key				Assessment guide
25–24 = A+	19 = B+	14 = C+	10 = D	5 = Advanced
23–21 = A	18–16 = B	13–12 = C	9 = D–	4 = Proficient
20 = A–	15 = B–	11 = C–		3 = Basic
				2 = Below Basic
				1 = Novice

Date _____

Strategies for Differentiating in the Content Areas © 2007 by Beverly Strayer and Troy Strayer, Scholastic Teaching Resources

CHAPTER 7

Employing Terminology Tactics

CONTENT OBJECTIVE:
Students attach meaning to and retain content-area vocabulary words.

DIFFERENTIATION APPROACH:
Vary the processes students use to learn vocabulary.

In every content area class, students are introduced to a plethora of vocabulary words that are essential to understanding and to making meaning of the content. Just think—if students were to learn two new words per period in an eight-period school day, they would be responsible for learning 16 new vocabulary words each day. In a matter of one week students would be expected to learn 80 new words! How can we best help students accomplish all this?

Traditional strategies, such as copying down the definition of a new term from the textbook glossary or a dictionary, require students to take in information passively. It's no wonder so many students get frustrated when they can't recall this information a week later on a traditional paper and pencil test. Students usually can't learn the word and its meaning well enough with such a limited, unengaged experience. In fact, we now know that our students learn best when they interact with words and ideas, tie new learning into their prior knowledge, and internalize—rather than memorize—meanings and concepts. The vocabulary-learning strategies in this chapter allow students to make meaning of complex vocabulary terms by tapping their interests and learning-style preferences and helping them to make a personal connection with these words. In turn, students' understanding of vocabulary increases and thus, their understanding of the topics they study deepens. Their confidence in the subject matter builds as well.

These terminology tactics can be used as independent practice or as pre-assessments, formative assessments, and summative assessments. As a pre-assessment to a new unit, these tools help you identify what ideas and concepts students know and what background they may bring to the unit. During the unit of study, you can assess your students with one of these tools to evaluate their understanding of the unit's vocabulary terms, and then reteach as needed. Following a unit of study, terminology tactics can serve as a summative assessment to show that your students have mastered the content.

Terminology Tactic 1: Word Blasts

This quick-to-complete organizer taps multiple intelligence areas (visual-spatial, logical-mathematical, and verbal-linguistic engagement) to help students build strong connections with the target word.

Materials

- Word Blast template (page 86)
- list of vocabulary words you're ready to review
- (optional) materials that can draw attention to key ideas and help students with their sketches, such as colored pencils, highlighters, sticky notes, or rulers

Procedure

1. Distribute copies of the Word Blast template and have students fill in the target words you've selected. (We recommend starting with just two to four words—interacting with too many words at once may overwhelm some students.)

2. Point out that the Word Blast is broken into four information quadrants with the vocabulary word in the center (see the life-science Word Blast on page 82). Adapt the format to meet the needs of the assignment or your students, as shown in the American Revolution example (page 89), which asks a focused, higher-level question for each term ("How did this impact the Revolution?"), in place of the student-generated sentence. Encourage

> Teaching vocabulary terms had been a frustrating part of the curriculum for us until we learned about and began to use these tactics. Now, it's an enjoyable piece of our work; students make personal connections with the words and more easily retain their meanings. Most important, they are motivated to learn new vocabulary. Pulling out a tactic sets off a spark in the classroom.

students to use available resources, such as the textbook, the Internet, their notes, and class activities, to explore each new word. You may want to complete the first Word Blast together and then let students tackle the rest for independent work.

3. To help students use the Word Blasts as a study tool, have them cut each one out and staple the sheets together so that are looking at only one word at a time.

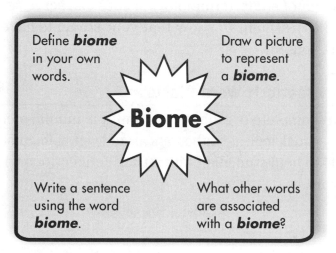

Terminology Tactic 2: Word Art

Using the letters of the topic name, students create illustrations about the topic. This artwork engages everyone and often elicits very detailed, information-rich products from learners with visual and spatial strengths.

Materials

- sheets of white copy paper
- one or more key words or concepts from the unit/lesson
- optional materials listed for Tactic 1

Procedure

1. Assign or have students choose a key term or concept from the unit you're studying, such as *evolution, operations, setting,* or *immigration.* This strategy requires time and creativity, so either plan a full period or allow students some time to get started in class and then have them complete it for homework.

2. Have students define the term in their own words. (This might begin with notes on a notebook page followed by a peer discussion.)

3. Encourage students to show this definition by using their artistic and visual skills to represent the word, letter by letter, on a blank page. You might show them the astronomy word art example on page 90.

4. Have students share the completed examples. Comparing and contrasting how their peers captured the meaning of the word will help deepen their understanding.

5. You may want to have students polish and copy their word art pieces—they make an eye-catching display.

Terminology Tactic 3: Mix and Match

Students love moving around the room and interacting with their peers as they match words to definitions and then discuss the meaning. This is a great activity for kinesthetic and auditory engagement.

A student puts the finishing touches on her word art piece before the bell rings.

Materials

- Mix and Match template (page 87)
- list of vocabulary words you're ready to review

Procedure

1. Select a set of vocabulary words students need to review. The number of words should equal half the number of students in your class.

2. On copies of the Mix and Match template, write the words on the "Word" cards and their meanings on the "Definition" cards. (To increase complexity, attach a picture to the "Word" card in place of the vocabulary term. Students will have to figure out which vocabulary term the picture represents.) Cut out and laminate the completed cards for durability. (You may want to print the words and definitions on index cards in lieu of the template.)

3. Distribute the cards—both words and definitions—randomly so that every student has a card.

4. Review the task with students: On your signal, they are to walk around the room quietly, showing their card to their peers and looking for the card that matches the one they're holding. When they find the peer with the matching card, they are responsible for working together for a few minutes on two items that they will present to the group. First, they must correctly pronounce the word and state its definition in their own words. Second, they must come up with a meaningful sentence that uses the word as it relates to their studies.

5. Collect, shuffle, and redistribute the cards. By repeating this activity several times with the same cards, students hear multiple examples of their vocabulary words used in context and develop their own examples for several target words.

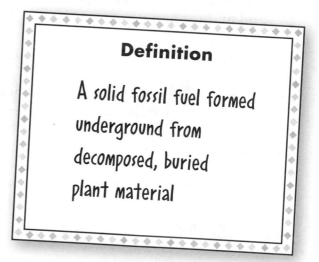

Sentence:

We heat our house over the winter by using **coal** in our stove.

Terminology Tactic 4: Word Branching

Students use an organizer to examine the meaning of a word from several angles, which engages their logical and verbal-linguistic intelligences. The completed Word Branch makes a great study aid.

Materials

- Word Branching template (page 88)
- list of vocabulary words you're ready to review
- text(s) in which the words are located

Procedure

1. Distribute copies of the Word Branching template and have students fill in the target word you've selected. (As with Word Blasts, we recommend starting with two to four words—interacting with too many words at once may overwhelm some students.)

2. Have students interact with the word from three different perspectives and write their responses on the form. They will:
   - Use context clues from the text to formulate a definition of the vocabulary term. (Make sure students have the reading materials they need to locate and reread the passages with the target words.) Have them come up with two possibilities for the word's meaning. These examples may be written or drawn, depending on the preference of the student.
   - Apply the vocabulary term to the subject matter. Based on their prior knowledge or use of context clues, students provide two examples of how this term relates to the subject matter being learned. Again, these examples may be written or drawn depending on the preference of the student.
   - Using what they've learned about the word, generate related words, listing similar terms or concepts.

3. As students compare their definitions, examples, and related words, they can refine their ideas. To further increase their interaction with the words, have students work in pairs to list all their related terms in order of how closely related they are to the original term.

Word Blast

Define _____ in your own words.

Draw a picture to represent _____.

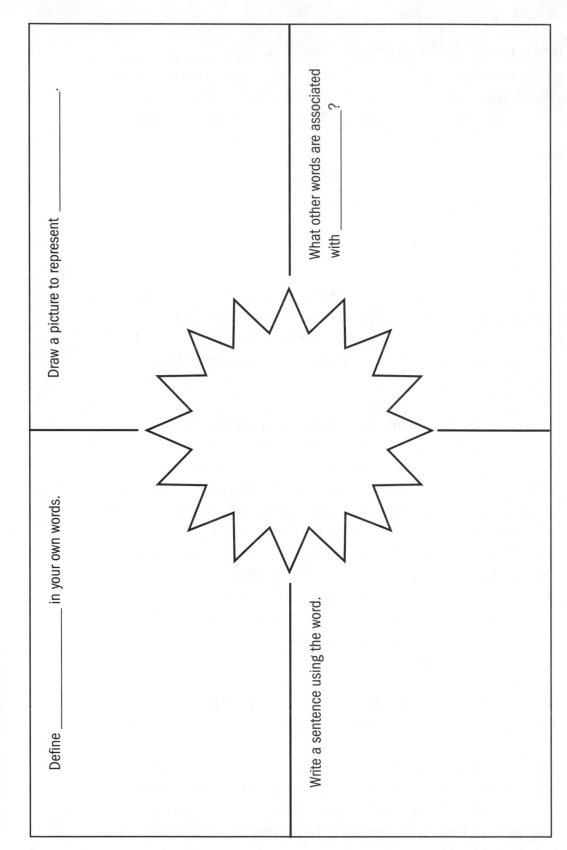

Write a sentence using the word.

What other words are associated with _____?

Mix and Match

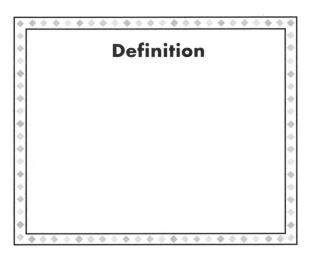

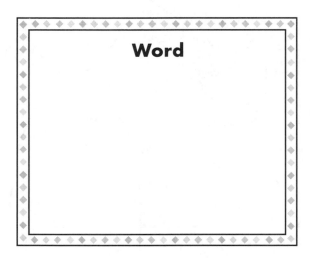

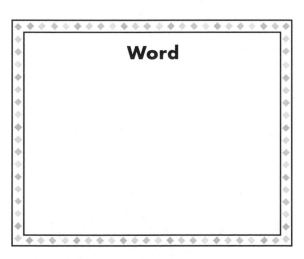

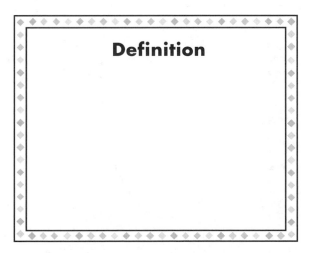

Word Branching

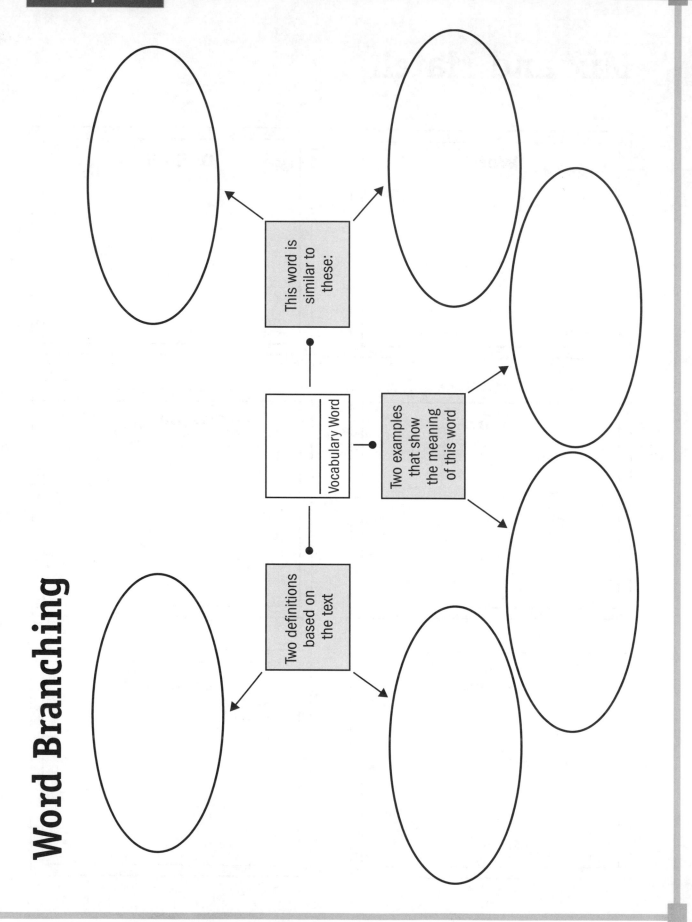

This word is similar to these:

Vocabulary Word

Two examples that show the meaning of this word

Two definitions based on the text

Word Blast

(Social Studies, American Revolution)

ASSIGNMENT NOTES:

In this example, the student explored terms relating to the American Revolution, including a group of people (Green Mountain Boys), a battle site (Bunker Hill), and an important contemporary document (*Common Sense*). The assignment tied the glossary definition to a memorable image, and provided the student's evaluation of how the term related to the revolution. The Word Blast becomes part of her study materials for the unit.

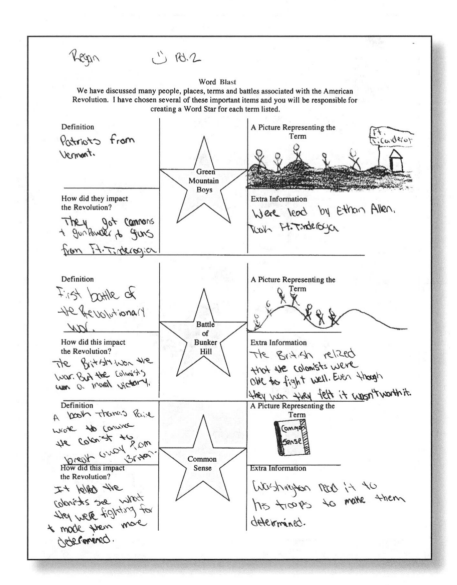

Word Art

(Earth Science, Astronomy)

ASSIGNMENT NOTES:

Following a lesson on the definition and characteristics of astronomy in an earth science class, students were asked to complete a word art piece showing their understanding of the term and the concepts associated with astronomy. In this example, the student took the letters and shaped them into personal examples of how she conceptualized *astronomy*.

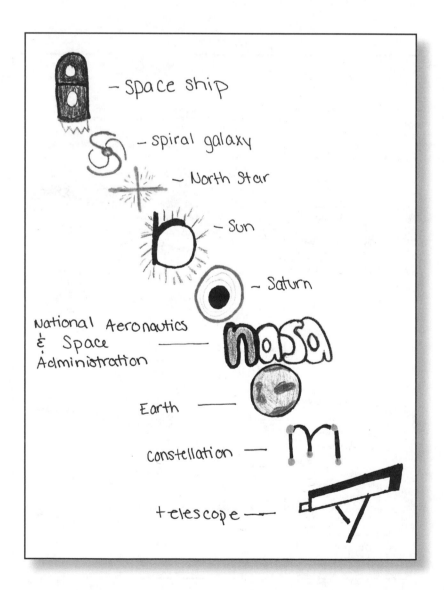

Word Branching

(Biology, Cell Function and Structure)

ASSIGNMENT NOTES:

This biology student shows what she's learned about the structure
and function of the nucleus in this word branching assignment.
She uses words and a picture to give the definition, describes
key functions in the examples, and chooses an associated phrase
(*control center*) and an excellent analogy (*company headquarters*)
to convey the importance and role of the nucleus.

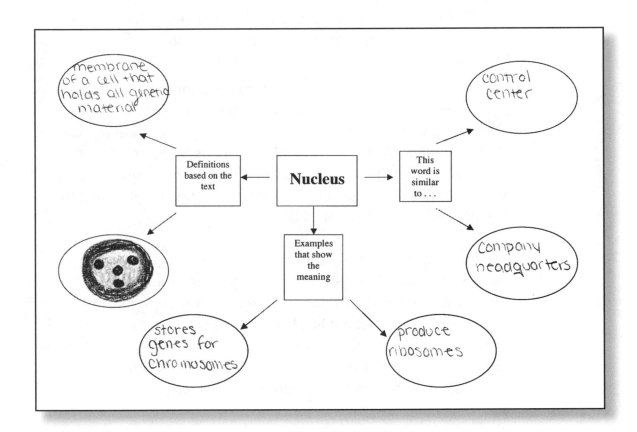

CHAPTER 8

Providing Closure

CONTENT OBJECTIVE:
> At the close of a lesson, students demonstrate in detail what they know about a specific lesson objective.

DIFFERENTIATION APPROACH:
> Tap students' interests and learning styles to help them create products that recap what they've learned.

In the late 1970s, Madeline Hunter researched the teaching strategies of effective educators. She found that one strategy these educators often used was having students summarize the daily lesson, a practice commonly known as "closure." Classroom research has proven that closure helps students retain what was learned and also assists students in transferring the learning to life beyond the classroom walls.

Closure is a critical part of *every* lesson—not only for students, but also for you. When students attempt to summarize the key ideas and apply skills learned in a lesson, you discover how successful your teaching has been. With this daily assessment of your students' learning comes an opportunity for you to reflect on and improve instruction. In turn, closure activities allow students to revisit the objective and solidify the learning for the day.

Not only does closure provide an assessment for the completed lesson, it also serves as a pre-assessment for the next day's lesson. For example, you wouldn't want to move on to a lesson covering the division of cells if students are still having trouble with identifying the key functions of cell parts, the objective of the lesson you just taught—they'd be lost. Using data from the closure activity to plan the next day's lesson gives you the opportunity to encourage students who demonstrate a satisfactory understanding of the objective in their closure responses to move on to an anchor activity (see Chapter 1) while you clarify any misconceptions about the previous day's learning for those who need reteaching.

Time spent on closure is time well spent. We save time and energy and increase enthusiasm for learning when we make sure no students are left behind. In fact, when you implement closure activities regularly in your classroom, students will remind you if you forget to do it. They will value the opportunity to demonstrate what they have learned or let you know where they may be confused. As we often say, "Whatever is worth teaching is worth closing."

Closure Activity 1: 3-2-1 Review

This tool helps students generate a quick, targeted, and easy-to-read response to your lesson in a format they enjoy. It also highlights any misconceptions or confusion students may have about what they've heard or read during the lesson. For a variation on this format, see Closure Activity 4: Triangle-Square-Circle.

Materials

• 3-2-1 Review template (page 102)

Procedure

1. As you plan your lesson, fill in the 3, 2, and 1 sections on the template in a way that prompts students to state key information and ideas from the lesson. The prompts should help students list three things learned during the lesson, two things they would feel comfortable teaching others, and one thing that still isn't clear. For example, a closure for an introductory lesson on European colonization of the New World might ask students to:
    a. Name *three* reasons that the European settlers came to the New World.
    b. Write *two* things you've learned about the settlers that you could teach to your classmates.
    c. Write *one* thing that you would like to have someone explain to you. (See the example on page 108.)

O f all the strategies we've presented, we're most committed to providing closure for our lessons. Closure activities help kids fully digest the ideas and information we've presented and show us what we need to reteach. Because we want to keep our closures interesting for students, we are careful not to use the same activity repeatedly. Each week we draw from the ideas presented here to develop five closure activities that address different learning styles and interests. This way, at least once a week, each student's learning style preferences or interests are fully engaged at the lesson's closing.

2. Distribute copies of the 3-2-1 Review page you've made at the end of your lesson, allowing 3–5 minutes for students to complete it.

3. After class, check that all students have responded appropriately. Gather responses from students who may have missed key ideas or have questions that show they need reinforcement or clarification. This will help you plan for the next lesson or for individual or small-group reteaching.

Closure Activity 2: A-B Conversation

As students practice brainstorming and paraphrasing, they review what they have learned, while honing their summarization skills. For a more sophisticated version of this activity, see Closure Activity 8: Turn Three/Four Review (page 99).

Materials

- (none needed)

Procedure

1. Group students in pairs and assign partners the role of "A" or "B."

2. *A* must present everything that he or she has learned from the lesson in 90 seconds. *B* has to listen carefully and paraphrase everything that *A* says. (See prompts on the next page.)

3. To give students a chance to try both roles, identify two topics discussed during the lesson. Let *A* present and *B* paraphrase on the first topic and then have them switch roles for the second topic.

4. Once partners are finished, have a few pairs share their presentation/paraphrasing with the class. Ask students to agree or disagree by nodding "yes" or shaking their heads "no." Encourage students to explain with specific examples why they disagree. (Note: Make sure that students are sharing accurate information. It is important that students understand the skill of paraphrasing. You will be able to evaluate what they have learned when you ask the pairs to share and the others to agree or disagree.)

PROMPTS FOR A–B CONVERSATIONS:

FOR MATH:
Partner A: Explain to Partner B how to find the area of a triangle. You have 90 seconds.
Partner B: Paraphrase what Partner A said.

FOR SCIENCE:
Partner B: Describe the climate and vegetation of the Taiga Biome to Partner A.
Partner A: Paraphrase what Partner B said.

FOR HEALTH:
Partner A: Describe the food pyramid to Partner B.
Partner B: Paraphrase what Partner A said. Also, discuss the reasons that fruits and vegetables are important in our diet.

FOR SOCIAL STUDIES:
Partner B: Explain the importance of the Battle of Lexington and Concord in the development of the Revolutionary War to Partner A.
Partner A: Paraphrase what Partner B said.

Closure Activity 3: Make a List

Students make a simple list of ideas and concepts they've learned and take it through several rounds of revision, refining their ideas through peer interactions in groups of different sizes until a master list is created for the class.

Materials

- scrap paper or notebooks
- chart paper and a marker

Procedure

1. Have students work in pairs to make a list of ideas and skills they've learned during the lesson or unit. They may write the list in their notebooks or on scrap paper.

2. After a few minutes, have students share the list with another pair and add to or revise it, creating a new, group list. This process helps students recall concepts or ideas they may have

forgotten and also to clarify misunderstandings. Help students find a way to share the task so that everyone in the group is involved. For example, in an American history class, two pairs of students form a group and decide that each member will select his or her three best ideas from the original lists to create a new, improved list of key points about the Liberty Bell. They initial each line to show their contributions. The list includes:

   a. Weighs 2080 lbs.–*BN*
   b. Arrived on Sept. 1, 1752 –*SV*
   c. Bell raised on March 29, 1753 –*SP*
   d. British wanted to melt the bell because it symbolized independence –*MD*
   e. Raised and fixed on June 11, 1753 –*BN*
   f. Tolled on repeal of Sugar Act in 1764 –*SV*
   g. Muffled and tolled on announcement of Stamp Act in 1765 –*SP*
   h. Loudest tolling on July 8, 1776 –*MD*

3. Have the groups of four elect a member to present their list to the class. Make a master list on large chart paper as the groups present. Take at least two things learned from each group of four. (This list can be hung in the room for future reference.) Students are usually amazed at how much they have learned in a period.

Closure Activity 4: Triangle-Square-Circle

In addition to providing evidence of what students have learned, this activity provides a safe platform for students to ask questions about parts of the lesson that confuse them—questions that they may be embarrassed to ask in front of their peers. This is a great tool for targeting specific needs and misunderstandings. (See also Closure Activity 1: 3-2-1 Review.)

Materials

   • Triangle-Square-Circle template (page 103)

Procedure

1. Distribute copies of the Triangle-Square-Circle template. (You may also have students copy the shapes on notebook paper from an overhead transparency image.)
2. Give students the following directions:

- Write three things you learned, one on each corner of the triangle.
- In the square, write two things that "square" with what you already knew.
- In the circle, write a question you still have about what you learned.
  (See the full example on page 109.)

3. Collect students' responses. You should be able to quickly evaluate what students have learned, how familiar they are with the topic, and whether they have misconceptions about the material. Their questions can help prepare you for beginning the next lesson.

Closure Activity 5: $1.00 Summary

Use this summarization exercise to help students write about the main idea of the lesson effectively and efficiently. Once they have learned this strategy, they will be able to summarize the day's lesson in 20 words or less, providing you with a quick overview of what each student has taken from the lesson.

Materials

- $1.00 Summary template (page 104)
- students' notes or class notes

Procedure

1. At the end of the lesson, let students take a couple of minutes to review their notes and underline important words and main ideas.

2. Distribute copies of the $1.00 Summary template and have students fill in the sheet with the lesson objective and important words (words related to the main idea). Have them use this word bank to write a 20-word summary of the lesson at the bottom of the page. Tell them to imagine that they have $1.00 and each word used will cost $.05. When they reach 20 words, they're out of money. (See the example on page 110.)

Closure Activity 6: Magic Border

This drawing-based activity motivates students who are strong visual-spatial learners. It allows them to demonstrate what they have learned in a form other than the written word and often stimulates very creative responses. By providing details in their sketches, they can show a substantial amount of information.

Materials

- Magic Border template (page 105) or copy paper

Procedure

1. Distribute copies of the Magic Border template or have students trace a one-inch border on a sheet of copy paper. In the middle of the paper, have them copy the "big idea" of the day's lesson.

2. Inside the border, have students draw pictures or symbols that support the big idea. Assure students that stick drawings are perfectly acceptable. They may also add important words, grafitti-style. (See the examples on page 111.)

3. In addition to showing you concrete evidence of what students have taken away from the lesson, these borders can be displayed on a board or brought out to review key ideas and words before moving on to the next lesson.

Closure Activity 7: Bend, Twist, Represent!

This quick and easy activity is a big hit with middle and high school students. Even better, the critical thinking this strategy stimulates is phenomenal! Students are actually moving to the analysis and synthesis levels of Bloom's Taxonomy as they make a simple, three-dimensional representation of their learning, and they feel comfortable sharing their creations with others. Those who may not excel at writing can demonstrate their learning without ever picking up a pencil or touching paper.

Materials

- two or more chenille stems per student (Note: Students tend to prefer using two different-color stems. The colored ones from craft shops or dollar stores work well.)

Procedure

1. At the close of the lesson, give students two chenille stems and ask them to use the stems to visually represent what they have learned.

2. After about 90 seconds, have them think about how they will explain their representation to their peers.

3. Let students meet in groups of three or four, show their chenille stem creations, and tell how their creations represent what they've learned.

4. Have one or two students from each group share some of the best features from the creations in their group.

5. Have students straighten the chenille stems, and collect them so they may be reused.

A representation of how disagreements over taxation and government, distance, and eventually war, unraveled the connection between the Colonies and England

Closure Activity 8: Turn Three/Four Review

Though students work in groups to complete the Turn Three (or Turn Four) Review, each participates in answering all the lesson-review questions you pose. Students take turns generating the answer, paraphrasing the answer, or checking and recording the answer. Madeline Hunter believed that "every student should answer every question, every time." This activity makes sure that every student is involved in some meaningful way with every question. And the work is differentiated: The student's job on every question changes.

Materials

- Turn Three or Turn Four Review template (pages 106–107)
- copy paper

Procedure

1. Before your lesson, select three or four questions or response prompts that will help students demonstrate their learning. Write the questions into the Turn Three/Four Review template(s). (The Turn Four template requires four questions and is used with groups of four; the Turn Three template requires three questions and is used with groups of three, as shown with the assignment sheet below.) Make enough copies of the review sheet you've created for the number of groups you'll have.

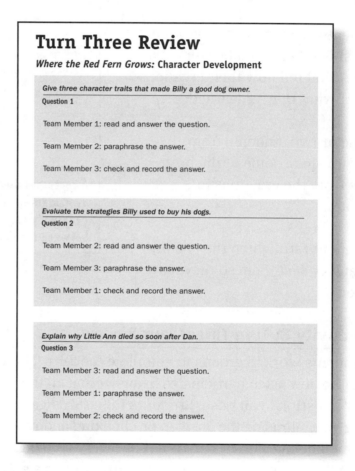

Turn Three Review

Where the Red Fern Grows: Character Development

Give three character traits that made Billy a good dog owner.
Question 1

Team Member 1: read and answer the question.

Team Member 2: paraphrase the answer.

Team Member 3: check and record the answer.

Evaluate the strategies Billy used to buy his dogs.
Question 2

Team Member 2: read and answer the question.

Team Member 3: paraphrase the answer.

Team Member 1: check and record the answer.

Explain why Little Ann died so soon after Dan.
Question 3

Team Member 3: read and answer the question.

Team Member 1: paraphrase the answer.

Team Member 2: check and record the answer.

2. At the end of the lesson, group students according to your plans and have group members number off, so that each student has a number: 1, 2, and 3 or 1, 2, 3, and 4.

3. Distribute a question sheet and a blank answer sheet to each group. Review the roles each group member plays in answering the questions; each person in the group is required to do a different job each time a new question is read. As students contribute to the review by generating the answer, paraphrasing it,

checking it, and recording it, encourage them to ask one another for clarification and offer suggestions. They may return to their notes or reading for support. A conversation might begin like this:

QUESTION 1
(Team member 1 reads and answers the prompt)

David: "Give three character traits that made Billy a good dog owner." . . . Billy was loyal, loving, and hard-working with his dogs.

(Team member 2 paraphrases the answer)

Howard: Billy cared about his dogs, worked hard training them to hunt, and stuck with them no matter what.

(Team member 3 checks and records the answer)

Stacey: I agree with your answers.
(*Stacey records the answer David gave.*)

QUESTION 2
(Team member 2 reads and answers the prompt)

Howard: "Evaluate the strategies Billy used to buy his dogs." . . . I think Billy was smart and worked hard to make the money to buy the dogs. He also walked miles and miles to get the dogs.

(Team member 3 paraphrases the answer)

Stacey: Billy earned the money to pay for his dogs, and he didn't bother his parents. He walked barefoot to a town far away to pick them up.

(Team member 1 checks and records the answer)

David: Howard, you gave good answers.
(*David records the answer Howard gave.*)

At this point students would switch roles once more to answer question 3.

4. Before you collect the answer sheets, make sure students have marked which role they played and have provided complete answers for every question. The answer sheet provides you with feedback for planning your next lesson.

3-2-1 Review

3. _____

   1. _____

     _____

     _____

   2. _____

     _____

     _____

   3. _____

     _____

     _____

2. _____

   1. _____

     _____

     _____

   2. _____

     _____

     _____

1. _____

   1. _____

     _____

     _____

Triangle-Square-Circle

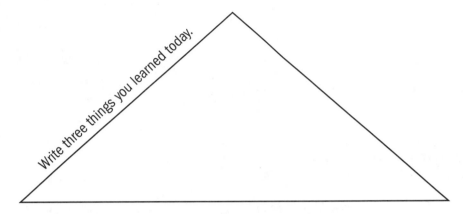

Write three things you learned today.

Write two things that "square"
with what you already knew.

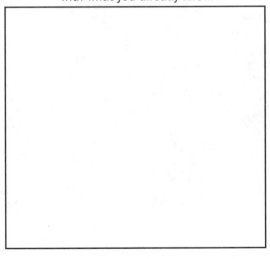

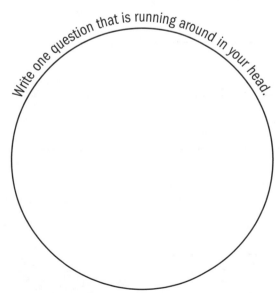

Write one question that is running around in your head.

$1.00 Summary

Lesson Objective

Important/Main Idea Words

$1.00 Summary

_____   _____   _____   _____

_____   _____   _____   _____

_____   _____   _____   _____

_____   _____   _____   _____

_____   _____   _____   _____

Magic Border

Turn Three Review

Question 1

Team Member 1: read and answer the question.

Team Member 2: paraphrase the answer.

Team Member 3: check and record the answer.

Question 2

Team Member 2: read and answer the question.

Team Member 3: paraphrase the answer.

Team Member 1: check and record the answer.

Question 3

Team Member 3: read and answer the question.

Team Member 1: paraphrase the answer.

Team Member 2: check and record the answer.

Turn Four Review

Question 1

Team Member 1: read and answer the question.

Team Member 2: paraphrase the answer.

Team Member 3: check the answer.

Team Member 4: record the answer.

Question 2

Team Member 2: read and answer the question.

Team Member 3: paraphrase the answer.

Team Member 4: check the answer.

Team Member 1: record the answer.

Question 3

Team Member 3: read and answer the question.

Team Member 4: paraphrase the answer.

Team Member 1: check the answer.

Team Member 2: record the answer.

Question 4

Team Member 4: read and answer the question.

Team Member 1: paraphrase the answer.

Team Member 2: check the answer.

Team Member 3: record the answer.

3-2-1 Review

(Social Studies, European Colonization of the New World)

ASSIGNMENT NOTES:

This quick-check closure activity was typed up and given to students at the end of class to make sure they had understood key reasons for European settlement and motivations of the settlers. Jaime's response shows that he's understood why settlers left for a new life and suggests that he's interested in the fate of "The Lost Colony," which might be a direction for anchor activity research.

3-2-1 Review

Jaime
10/12

3   Name three reasons that the European settlers came to the New World.

1. gold
2. God
3. glory

2   Write two things you've learned about the settlers that you could teach your classmates.

1. I learned that most of them came because of religion.
2. Also Roanoke was the first real settlement.

1   Write one thing that you would like to have someone explain to you.

1. What happened to the settlers at Roanoke?

Triangle-Square-Circle

(Geometry, Area and Perimeter)

ASSIGNMENT NOTES:

After three days of lessons on area and perimeter, I asked students to complete a Triangle-Square-Circle closure activity to determine what they had learned and which concepts still were giving them trouble. Below, a fifth-grade student completed this example of a Triangle-Square-Circle Closure activity on area and perimeter of rectangles, parallelograms, and circles.

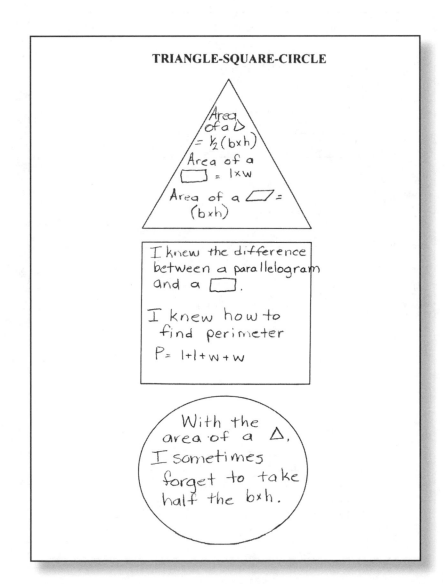

$1.00 Summary

(Life Sciences, Biomes)

ASSIGNMENT NOTES:

During a study of biomes in fifth grade science class, students were asked to provide a $1.00 Summary and a description of biomes. These summaries help students use concise language. At the conclusion of the lesson, and after reading the science text, Ronni provided this 20-word summary.

$1.00 Summary

Name	Date 11/14/06
Lesson Objective: Students will be able to define and describe biomes	

Important/Main Idea Words

* Area of plant and animal groups that adapted to environment.
* climate + geography determine biome.
* Any change in climate changes the biome.
* All plants + animals depend on each other.
* humans can change a biome.
* there are 6 major biomes.
* we should work to preserve biomes.

$1.00 Summary

Biomes,	determined	by	climate
and	geography,	have	plants
and	animals.	we	should
save	biomes.	Plants	and
animals	need	each	other.

Magic Border

(American History, Liberty Bell)

ASSIGNMENT NOTES:

To help students process their learning from our annual field trip to Philadelphia, we used the Magic Border closure activity. Students loved showing what they learned about the Liberty Bell by illustrating the border around its name. As the examples below show, our students learned many interesting facts and enjoyed representing in pictures and words what they had learned.

Bibliography

Rawls, W. (1974). *Where the red fern grows*. New York: Bantam.

Schoessler, P. (2002). *Differentiated instruction*. Exton, PA: Chester County Intermediate Unit, Chester County Schools.

Tomlinson, C. A. (1999). *The differentiated classroom: Responding to the needs of all learners*. Alexandria, VA: Association for Supervision and Curriculum Development.

Tomlinson, C. A. (2001). *How to differentiate instruction in mixed ability classrooms*. Alexandria, VA: Association for Supervision and Curriculum Development.